The Entrepreneurial Dynamics in Italy

Alessandra Micozzi

The Entrepreneurial Dynamics in Italy

A Focus on Academic Spin-Offs

palgrave
macmillan

Alessandra Micozzi
Centre for Innovation
and Entrepreneurship
Polytechnic University of Marche
Novedrate, Como, Italy

ISBN 978-3-030-55182-7 ISBN 978-3-030-55183-4 (eBook)
https://doi.org/10.1007/978-3-030-55183-4

This Palgrave Macmillan imprint is published by the registered company Springer Nature Switzerland AG
The registered company address is: Gewerbestrasse 11, 6330 Cham, Switzerland

To a great entrepreneur, my father
To his magical helper, my mother

Preface I

This book was written to honor all those who, with patience and dedication, capture opportunities and find the courage to enhance their intuitions: my father and mother, who create any color you can imagine and have succeeded, with the help of Marco, to transform a family business into a jewel of professionalism and efficiency; Francesca, with whom we have helped many aspiring entrepreneurs to start their businesses; Andrea, who from commander of the Navy, has transformed the family land into a beautiful farm; Piero and Maria, who create instruments to turn sound into emotion; Michele, who has founded an educational community for anyone who is ready to awaken the deeper part of himself; Giovanni, who extracts the energy of nature from plants and gives it to us in his phytotherapy; Francesca, who with her horses makes the life of the disabled more colourful; Riccardo, who spreads forgotten millennia knowledge in the modern era of digital communication; Giulia, my first partner, with whom we concluded the first crowdfunding campaign in our Region; Ivan, Luca and Patrick with whom we made an amazing functional chocolate; my students with the light of creativity in their eyes (Silvio, Massimo, Ale, Davide, Gian, Marius), and the other 1000 and 1 entrepreneurs or nascent entrepreneurs that I have found in my life.

A deep thanks to all of them who have been a source of inspiration for me: from Gabriele to Alberto, to Andrea up to Professor Balloni, thanks to whom I started my academic career under the guidance of Donato, my mentor in scientific research and a great example of humanity and competence, qualities difficult to find in the same person.

Special thanks to Chiara for her loving and precious help.

The biggest thanks go to my daughter Sara who brings out the best part of me.

Ancona, Italy Alessandra Micozzi

Preface II

Questo libro nasce per onorare tutti coloro che, con pazienza e dedizioni, colgono delle opportunità e trovano il coraggio per valorizzare le proprie intuizioni: mio padre e mia madre, che sanno realizzare qualsiasi colore si possa immaginare e sono riusciti, con l'aiuto di Marco, a trasformare un'impresa di famiglia in un gioiello di professionalità ed efficienza; Francesca, con cui abbiamo aiutato tanti aspiranti imprenditori ad attivare le loro imprese; Andrea, che da comandante della Marina Militare, ha trasformato i terreni di famiglia in una stupenda azienda Agricola; Piero e Maria, che riescono a trasformare il suono in emozione, Michele; che ha fondato una comunità educante per chiunque sia pronto a risvegliare la parte più profonda di se; Giovanni, che estrae dalle piante l'energia della natura e ce la dona nei suoi fitoterapici; Francesca, che con i suoi cavalli rende più colorata la vita dei disabili; Riccardo, che nella moderna era della comunicazione digitale diffonde conoscenze millenarie oramai dimenticate; Giulia, la mia prima socia, con cui abbiamo concluso la prima campagna di crowdfunding nella nostra Regione; Ivan, Luca e Patrick con i quali abbiamo realizzato uno strepitoso cioccolato funzionale; i miei studenti con la luce dell'intraprendenza negli occhi (Silvio, Massimo, Ale, Davide, Gian, Marius), e gli altri 1000 e 1 imprenditori o nascenti imprenditori che ho trovato nel mio cammino.

Un ringraziamento profondo a tutti coloro che sono stati per me fonte di ispirazione: da Gabriele ad Alberto, ad Andrea fino ad arrivare al professor Balloni, grazie al quale ho intrapreso la carriera accademica sotto la guida di Donato, mio mentore nella ricerca scientifica e grande esempio di umanità e competenza, doti difficili da trovare in una stessa persona.

Un ringraziamento speciale a Chiara per il suo amorevole e prezioso aiuto.

Il ringraziamento più grande va a mia figlia Sara che è riuscita a far emergere la parte migliore di me.

Novedrate, Italy Alessandra Micozzi

About This Book

New firm creation is one of the most important features of modern economic life. The emergence of new ventures is central to economic adaptation and change and one of the major factors associated with employment growth and increase in sector productivity. In addition, hundreds of millions pursue new firm creation as a serious career option. Knowing more about countries with different levels of firm creation, and the context and specific characteristics of those active in firm creation, is of considerable scientific, practical and policy interest (Reynolds, 2010; Acs et al., 2006).

Why is it important to focus on the dynamics of new initiatives?

The most significant is that new firms replenish and maintain the population of operating firms.

Second, new firms are the source of half of all new net job creation (Birch, 1987).

Third, the labour productivity of new firms is higher than existing and discontinuing businesses.

Fourth, new and small firms are a source of technical and market innovations (Audretsch, 1995).

Moreover, new firm creation is a major mechanism used by minorities to integrate themselves into the economy and, for many, a major route for status enhancement (Reynolds et al., 2004).

Last but not least, generally, entrepreneurship is attractive even for brilliant people with high levels of formal education who have difficulty in finding placement in existing organizations.

For all the above-mentioned reasons, entrepreneurship is now at the centre of many policy questions related to regional advantages, R&D, sustainability, human capital and employment. The stream of policy interest in entrepreneurship has fostered the growing academic interest in understanding the process and dynamics of entrepreneurship.

According to the literature, we can expect a positive relationship between the activation rate of new business initiatives and the overall growth of the economy, with reference to both entire countries and specific geographical areas.

Over the past decade, the entrepreneurial rate in Italy has decreased and the last GEM (Global Entrepreneurship Monitor) global report shows that Italy presents the lowest rate of total early stage entrepreneurial activities, defined as the prevalence rate of individuals in the working-age population who are involved in start-up activities, either in the phase preceding the birth of the firm (nascent entrepreneurs), or the phase spanning 42 months after the birth of the firm (new owner–managers of firms). Empirical evidence shows that the local production systems in Italy based on small firms have experienced increasing difficulty in ensuring the competitiveness of their production and the proper placement and remuneration of new recruits, in particular young people with a high level of education (D'Adda et al., 2020).

Several regions in advanced economies have experienced the same stagnation or decline in traditional manufacturing jobs and the changes in the patterns of entrepreneurial activity during the last decades pose a number of questions that satisfy both the objectives of scientific knowledge and the interests of policymakers who wish to implement measures for promoting entrepreneurship.

The main aim of this book is to provide a better understanding of the process for setting up new initiatives, analysing the multiple factors related to entrepreneurship dynamics.

Specifically, the first chapter analyses the factors explaining the entrepreneurial rates in Italy and the differences in entrepreneurial dynamics in a sample of EU countries.

From the methodological point of view, the following database is used:

- Movimprese for a descriptive analysis of entrepreneurial rates in Italy by year (from 2002 to 2019);
- Gem (Global Entrepreneurship Monitor) APS (adult population survey) to analyse the personal, business and environmental factors explaining the rate of nascent entrepreneurs.

The principal findings show that the entrepreneurial dynamics are very different across countries and in order to establish a policy to foster entrepreneurship, there is a need to investigate which factors drive the entrepreneurial process.

From a macroeconomic perspective, the ability of a country to support entrepreneurship is determined by conditions linked with context, while at a micro level, the likelihood of a person becoming an entrepreneur is influenced by individual personal traits, that determine the entrepreneur's response to entrepreneurial push or pull factors (loss of employment, discontent at work vs chance or opportunity to pursuit an idea).

Gender, age, level of education, social perception of self-employment as a good career choice have an impact on the probability to become a nascent entrepreneur but with different significance across countries and across sectors (low tech vs high-tech sectors) in the same countries.

Another important aspect is that very few nascent entrepreneurs in Italy start a business in high-tech sectors.

According to the endogenous growth theory, for which technological innovation is seen as the most important factor for achieving long-term economic growth, in Italy a change in the composition of production activities is needed, especially in the manufacturing sector, with a move towards productions which have a greater knowledge content (high-tech sectors). Regional policy in this area, prompted mainly by the availability of European funds, moves along two parallel tracks: on the one hand, to promote innovation within existing firms, and on the other to promote entrepreneurship in new areas of activity, especially in high technology sectors. In both cases there is a reassessment of the role of research centres and universities in technology transfer activity from these to industry.

For this reason, the second chapter is focused on the phenomenon of academic entrepreneurship that could be defined as the direct involvement of academic scientists in the development and commercialization of their research. The commercialization of scientific and technological knowledge produced within public research institutions such as universities, laboratories, research centres is increasingly considered by policy-makers as fuel for developing and sustaining regional economic growth and the most promising way to transfer research results to the market place is the creation of a new firm: the best way to do this is to set-up academic spin-offs.

The second chapter analyses the experience of Italian spin-offs, from their first introduction in 1999. Up to now empirical analyses of the phenomenon has focused on analysing the characteristics of spin-offs and their growth, the difference between those universities that have been most active in the creation of spin-offs and those that have been least active, the factors that foster the creation, the beneficial impact on the growth of other local high-tech start-ups when these are able to detect, absorb, and use this knowledge, etc.

After twenty years' experience of spin-off promotion by universities and local institutions, there is a growing concern about the evaluation of the impact of spin-offs on university technology transfer and local economies.

The empirical analysis refers to a sample of 210 Italian spin-offs set up between 2000 and 2006. From a quantitative point of view, measured by variables such as turnover or employment, the impact is rather marginal and this confirms the literature evidence which shows that most academic spin-offs are not gazelles: most of them start small and remain small, reflecting founder aspirations, capabilities and resource endowments. Several studies investigate the possible reasons to explain these: the imbalance of the sponsor team towards technical skills, lack of clarity in the identification of the entrepreneurial figure, the difficulty of promoters to transform the academic knowledge in management and organizational objectives. This does not imply that the firm's performances should be attributed only to the entrepreneurial characteristics: the technical knowledge of the founder-entrepreneur plays a crucial role during the first stage of the firm's life, but during the growth stage, a more complex set of resources is necessary to sustain the firm's activities, and the main issues regard availability of financial resources, organizational weaknesses, availability of specialized suppliers, availability of professional services. As regards the Italian institutional context, for example, the main problem is the difficulty for new firms to raise adequate funds during their start-up phase and subsequent development. The lack of these factors generates a vicious circle where the low level of investment and commitment creates low revenue and consequent scant capacity to stimulate employment, affecting the business size and the economic role played by academic spin-offs.

Given these quantitative results, there is a need for assessing the effective role played by these firms in an advanced economy. What I want to demonstrate in the second chapter is that the impact of spin-offs tends to be local as most spin-offs stay within the same geographical area as the institution from which they originate. To investigate the phenomenon of university spin-offs considering the specific context means to change the focus at local level, where I think the impact is relevant. Ample empirical literature findings support this line of research giving growing importance of knowledge spillovers from university research to industrial innovation.

To the best of my knowledge, little attention has been paid to evaluate the role of spin-offs on technology transfer activity by universities and to their impact on local systems. The aim of the second chapter is to cover this knowledge gap, developing an analytical framework to evaluate the impact of academic spin-offs on university technology transfer and regional development.

The empirical analysis is based on a sample of 26 spin-offs created between 2000 and 2010 from Università Politecnica delle Marche, for which balance sheet data and information about governance were examined. The analysis of the ownership and management team, and its change over time, was made through an examination of information provided by the Chambers of Commerce.

In order to develop a set of indicators to measure the impact of academic spin-offs, I chose to adopt a local approach due to the fact that there are several differences in the local innovation system and these may depend on the relevance of the three main actors of the triple helix model, university, industry and government, in terms of quantitative importance on the regional innovation system; orientation towards R&D and innovation; technology transfer activities by universities; the importance of relations between the three main actors; funds allocated by public institutions to firms and universities, etc. These differences in the local system determine the development of spin-offs. In this sense, the factors fostering the creation of this kind of firms are several. Regulations have an impact on spin-off activity because they determine the degree to which universities have the autonomy to make their own rules regarding technology transfer activities, like the reputation and research eminence of individual universities. Even the institutional factors such as culture of the university, its attitude towards spin-offs and the competence of the technology transfer office, could have an impact on this phenomenon. Moreover, the distribution of spin-offs across industry sectors is highly uneven and spin-offs are diverse in their activities because they reflect the prevalent sectors of research and activities of universities.

The empirical results reaffirm the consolidated literature about the localized nature of knowledge transfer. If knowledge spillover tends to occur only within limited geographic areas, embedding economic activity based on this knowledge within the local context, universities can become important focal points for local economic development.

In this sense, the main findings could be summarized as follows:

- The phenomenon of academic spin-offs could have a positive effect at the local level in terms of creation of high-tech entrepreneurship and employment and in terms of diffusion of technological spillover;
- There is a need to evaluate the phenomenon in the long term;
- The geographical span of the spin-off impact is mainly localized;
- In order to evaluate the real effect it is important to consider the local context in terms of industry specialization and policy objectives that have an important role in fostering the creation of new technology-based firms.

The chapters analyse also what factors affect the birth and the development of these companies: sectors of activities, geographical localization, ownership structure, the presence of a Technology Transfer Office (TTO) or business incubator and the presence of entrepreneurial courses at University.

The last factor is considered as particularly important because it could play an important role in fostering entrepreneurship, in general, and high-tech entrepreneurship, in particular, due to the lack of managerial and commercial skills of the nascent techno-entrepreneurs.

Bibliography

Acs, Z. J., & Szerb, L. (2006). Entrepreneurship, economic growth and public policy. *Small Business Economics, 28*(2–3), 109–122.

Audretsch, D. B. (1995). Firm profitability, growth, and innovation. *Review of Industrial Organization, 10*(5), 579–588.

Birch, D. L. (1987). *Job creation in America: How our smallest companies put the most people to work.* New York: Macmillan and Free Press.

D'Adda, D., Iacobucci, D., Micozzi, A., & Micozzi, F. (2020). *Rapporto Gem Italia 2019–2020*. Fabriano.

Reynolds, P. D. (2010). New firm creation: A global assessment of national, contextual, and individual factors. *ReVision, 6*(5–6), 315–496.

Reynolds, P. D., Carter, N., Gartner, W., & Greene, P. (2004). The prevalence of nascent entrepreneurs in the United States: Evidence from the panel study of entrepreneurial dynamics. *Small Business Economics, 23*(4), 263–284.

Contents

List of Figures

Chapter 1

Chapter 2

List of Tables

Chapter 2

CHAPTER 1

Entrepreneurial Dynamics

Abstract The creation of new business is seen as a key factor to reach economic goals at regional and national levels. Many regions in advanced countries have experienced stagnation or, in some cases, decline in traditional manufacturing sectors and the changes in the patterns of entrepreneurial activities towards innovation and knowledge are necessary. There is a need to understand the factors that have an impact on entrepreneurial dynamics, and the focus of this chapter is on the elements that foster or prevent entrepreneurship in Italy.

Keywords Entrepreneurship · New firms · Nascent entrepreneur

1 Introduction

In the past few decades, interest in the role of start-ups and small firms as determinants of employment growth and economic development has increased considerably. One of the reasons for this is that several regions in advanced economies have experienced stagnation or decline in traditional manufacturing activities. Stimulation of entrepreneurship and new business formation is viewed as a means to secure present and future job opportunities (Andersson & Noseleit, 2011).

There are strong reasons to believe that entrepreneurship is an essential explanatory factor of the economic performance of a country, and

A. Micozzi, *The Entrepreneurial Dynamics in Italy*,
https://doi.org/10.1007/978-3-030-55183-4_1

that the degree of productive entrepreneurial activity explains part of observed cross-country differences in economic performance (Davidsson & Henrekson, 2002). Entrepreneurship as a societal phenomenon draws attention to antecedents and outcomes of entrepreneurial behaviour, while entrepreneurship as a research field aims to understand what entrepreneurship is.

At policy level, recent documents by the European Commission (2010) and OECD (2010) (European Commission, 2011; OECD/EUROPEAN UNION, 2019) have emphasized the importance of entrepreneurship to promote the development of member countries.

In recent years, national and local governments have placed a great emphasis on the development of a culture of entrepreneurship, which is considered to be crucial for coping with the challenges and opportunities of globalization. The European Commission (EC) are stimulating entrepreneurship across all EU nations and regions, as a major driver of innovation, competitiveness and growth. This is being promoted and supported through a variety of strategies, policies, programmes and funds, structural and cohesion funds, focusing on improving the entrepreneurial environment for start-ups and existing firms.

Consequently, increasing the rate of new firm formation has become a key priority for policymakers interested in fostering economic development: "For a variety of reasons, promoting entrepreneurship enjoys support from governments at both ends of the political spectrum. Pro-entrepreneurship policies have been embraced as a means of increasing economic growth and diversity, ensuring competitive markets, helping the unemployed to generate additional jobs for themselves and others (rather than share existing work), countering poverty and welfare dependency, encouraging labour market flexibility, and drawing individuals out of informal economic activity. In short, an enterprise imperative has been charged with addressing a broad array of economic and social aspirations" (OECD, 2003, pp. 9–10).

National, regional and local policymakers are increasingly united in recognizing that economic growth is correlated with a favourable entrepreneurial environment and increasingly perceive the stimulation of a culture of entrepreneurship as a major politically driven task.

To implement effective entrepreneurship policies, it is necessary to understand the determinants of and the obstacles to entrepreneurship. The lack of internationally comparable empirical evidence and the fact that the measure of entrepreneurship is not a simple issue to prevent clear conclusions about the effectiveness of different policy approaches.

There is a consensus that entrepreneurship is a multifaceted concept that manifests itself in many different ways and, as a consequence, there are wide differences across academic disciplines about what entrepreneurship is (Salas-Fumas & Sanchez-Asin, 2013). Several definitions of entrepreneurship have emerged and measurement focuses on the individual level (self-employment) or firm level (business dynamics).

This first chapter is aimed at understanding the dynamics of new firm formation. In doing so it discusses the possible measures to analyse the entrepreneurial phenomenon, the factors affecting entrepreneurial dynamics and the factors explaining the national and regional differences in entrepreneurial rates.

The present chapter is organized as follows. The first section provides a critical review of the literature on entrepreneurship and entrepreneurial rates; the second one analyses the entrepreneurial dynamics in Italy during the period 2002–2019. Data about entrepreneurial rates are taken from the Movimprese database, provided by the Italian Chambers of Commerce. The second section investigates the differences in entrepreneurial dynamics among EU countries. The analysis is based on data from GEM (Global Entrepreneurship Monitor) that are available for the main European countries for the period 2001–2019. Differently from the Movimprese database, GEM data refers to the adult population rather than to firms. Moreover, they provide additional information on the personal characteristics of nascent and novice entrepreneurs and on the new venture they are going to implement (D'Adda, Iacobucci, Micozzi, & Micozzi, 2020).

2 Theoretical Background

2.1 Definition of Entrepreneurship

All concepts of entrepreneurship include the idea that a new business entity, activity, venture, product or service, has been created. The earliest use of the French word "entrepreneur" was associated with descriptions of those individuals assembling resources to produce new economic value.

Later development of the entrepreneurship concept emphasized a preference for risk-taking, opportunity recognition and exploitation, an orientation towards growth, or displacement of existing firms: the well-known "creative destruction" mechanism (Schumpeter, 1943). These views emphasize different aspects of entrepreneurship, but all include business creation as a central feature. While it is difficult to develop empirical measures of risk-taking or opportunity recognition or growth potential, it has been possible to develop reliable empirical measures of business creation.

Entrepreneurs are individuals who innovate, identify and create business opportunities, assemble and coordinate new combinations of resources so as to extract the most profit from their innovations in an uncertain context (Amit, Glosten, & Muller, 1993). Leibenstein (1968) offers a more detailed characterization of the entrepreneur as one who performs different tasks: (a) connects different markets; (b) answers a market gap; (c) creates and is responsible for contractual arrangements; (d) completes inputs and transforms them in outputs.

Schumpeter is the first author to address the question of the link between entrepreneurship and economic growth.

An increase in the number of entrepreneurs leads to an increase in economic growth. This effect is the result of the mobilization of their skills and their propensity to innovate. Schumpeter described this innovative activity as "the carrying out of new combinations", by distinguishing five cases: (1) the introduction of a new good or a new quality of a good; (2) the introduction of a new method of production; (3) the opening of a new market; (4) the occupation of a new source of supply of raw materials or half manufactured goods; (5) the carrying out of a new organization of industries, such as the creation of a monopoly position (Schumpeter, 2000).

By introducing new ideas, new processes, new products and services, Schumpeterian entrepreneurs affect and renew economic activities: the activities not only of the firms and industries, but also those of the region in which they are situated, generating economic growth.

Wennekers and Thurik (1999, p. 50) explicit this process: "At the aggregate level of industries, regions and national economies, the many individual entrepreneurial actions compose a mosaic of new experiments. In evolutionary terms this can be called variety. A process of competition between these various ideas and initiatives takes place continuously, leading to the selection of the most viable firms and industries. Variety, competition, selection and also imitation (...) expand and transform the productive potential of a regional or national economy (by replacement or displacement of obsolete firms, by higher productivity and by expansion of new niches and industries)".

The second author that shaped the economics literature on entrepreneurship in the twentieth century was Kirzner (1982). Entrepreneurs perceive profit opportunities and initiate actions to fill currently unsatisfied needs or to do more efficiently what is already done (Kirzner, 1985). In the Kirznerian tradition, entrepreneurs demonstrate inclination to exploit opportunities to generate profit.

Knight (1921) described the entrepreneur as one who undertakes uncertain investments, for which the future returns and the associated probability distribution are unknown. The entrepreneur is characterized as having an unusually low level of uncertainty aversion. Since the risks associated with entrepreneurial investments cannot be evaluated, they cannot be insured, and therefore the entrepreneur is the one who accepts to take these risks. Knight introduces the difference between risk and uncertainty. The uncertainty aversion, rather than risk aversion, is the major inhibitor mechanism of entrepreneurship. Estimating the degree to which a particular event is weighted with uncertainty, depends upon individual judgement expressed in terms of subjective probabilities. In this sense, a nascent entrepreneur is one who, based on his personal judgement, would accept to bear the uncertainty of production and market. Expected profits would be payment for this specific activity (Knight, 1921).

These three theoretical approaches to entrepreneurship began with the idea of studying the role of entrepreneurship in the economy. Moreover, they contributed to later development of entrepreneurship theory concerned with self-employment decisions. The latter approach is known as the theory of income choice. This approach has proved useful in describing some of the factors influencing the occupational choice. It is based on a neoclassical approach model where agents act as maximizers of expected utility. The occupational choice to become employees or entrepreneurs (self-employed) depends on the utility associated with the returns accruing from the two types of activity (Freytag & Thurik, 2007).

Several authors follow this approach by postulating differences across potential entrepreneurs in terms of some form of entrepreneurial attitudes (Lazear, 2005).

Other authors show that the degree of risk aversion and the differences in risk of the two occupational alternatives determine the occupational choice (Kihlstrom & Laffont, 1979): the less risk-averse individuals become entrepreneurs, while the more risk-averse ones choose to become employees.

Lucas comes closer to a Schumpeterian concept of entrepreneurship in the sense that, in his models, individuals do not differ in their attitude towards risk, but in their competence, intelligence and creative capacities (Lucas, 1978).

An interesting alternative to the expected utility model and in addition to low risk aversion of entrepreneurs, is the willingness and ability to handle ambiguity as well as other characteristics of entrepreneurs that are essential to the creation of successful new ventures (Bewley, 2002). These characteristics may include creativity, adaptability, technical know-how, vision and leadership ability, managerial and organizational skills, ability to make decisions quickly and to act in a rapidly changing and uncertain context, and a cultural background and formal education.

2.2 *The Theoretical Approaches to Entrepreneurship*

Several authors focus on entrepreneurship, assessing achievements, progress and future trends of the field, discussing methodological issues, concepts and research paradigms (Welter & Lasch, 2008).

In Europe, the number of entrepreneurship researchers at universities and research centres increased steadily over the 1980s and 1990s, which partly reflects a growing interest of governments in entrepreneurship themes.

The major questions which the entrepreneurship literature tries to answer are linked to the factors that affect why some new ventures succeed while others fail, the essence of entrepreneurship, the characteristics for which the probability to become a successful entrepreneur is high, the impact of market, rules and ecosystem in fostering entrepreneurial activities. Another question is: How and why do entrepreneurs decide to invest their time, talent and treasure (the three Ts of entrepreneurship) in their venture ideas? (Amit et al., 1993).

Several authors have tried to answer these questions. Specifically, a literature strand aims at identifying the factors affecting the choice to become an entrepreneur, while another strand aims at investigating the effect of entrepreneurship on economic growth.

2.2.1 *The Determinants of Self-Employment Choice*

Each of the theoretical approaches to entrepreneurship that we can study contains predictive and explanatory elements: social/cultural theory attempts to link entrepreneurship to the social and cultural context; personality-based theory suggests that specific psychological characteristics make people predisposed or not to entrepreneurship; network theory focuses on the social links and relationships which facilitate or constrain entrepreneurs; population ecology theory identifies environmental factors as the most important determinants of entrepreneurial success; finance theory focuses on capital markets to sustaining new ventures; and economic theory centres on analysis of market equilibrium in innovation and in new production processes, assuming that the entrepreneur is a rational actor (Dyer, 1994).

A large body of empirical research aims at identifying micro-level factors that can explain the formation and growth of new firms. Concerning formation phase, scholars identified a list of psychological and socio-demographic characteristics of business founders.

The first strand of literature concerns the "pull" factor that fosters entrepreneurial career. In this case, entry is a process generated by expectations of extra profits and hindered by barriers to entry (i.e. scale economies, cost of investment and specific sunk costs such as innovation or advertising expenditures) (Acs & Audretsch, 1989).

In this view, the dynamics towards market equilibrium in occupational choices—self-employed or employee—are guided by the equilibrium between profits and salaries. If the number of self-employed is too high, profits will be low and salaries will be high. As a consequence, some of the self-employed will become employees, so profits will increase, and salaries will decrease, to a new point of equilibrium where no individual wants to change occupation (Schjoedt & Shaver, 2007).

Lazear (2000) develops a model of choice between self-employment and employment, showing that the person who has a background in a large number of different roles (expressed in the number of different professional fields and professional degrees completed after school) has more probability of becoming an entrepreneur. Knowledge in different areas allows a nascent entrepreneur to put together the tangible and intangible resources needed for survival and success of a new business.

To become entrepreneur, Wagner (2004) focused on the importance of work experience in a small firm, which can be considered as a hothouse for nascent entrepreneurs. A vast number of empirical studies show that the start-up rate in a region seems to be positively related to the share of employees working in small firms (Audretsch & Fritsch, 1994a). In this view, working in a small firm tends to provide employees with a much more relevant experience for starting a new business, such as contacts with customers or with the owner of the firm who therefore provides a role model to follow.

On the pull side, the major motive for entrepreneurship is the feeling of freedom for both men and women, expressed by a desire for autonomy and control over one's life, that can represent the greatest source of satisfaction for men and women (Cromie & Hayes, 1988).

Another pull side factor is job satisfaction defined as "a pleasurable or positive emotional state resulting from the appraisal of one's job or job experiences" (Locke, 1976, p. 1300).

In this definition, job satisfaction is an attitude directly related to the experiences that a person undergoes during work. Thus, job dissatisfaction is a fundamental factor that motivates an individual to become an entrepreneur.

Some authors suggest that nascent entrepreneurs have developed certain perceptions in order to estimate their entrepreneurial abilities.

In this sense, individuals decide to start new ventures because they are confident in their abilities (self-efficacy), even when the probability of failure is high.

Carter, Gartner, Shaver, and Gatewood (2003) identified six categories of reasons for starting businesses:

1. Innovation, thus the intention of nascent entrepreneurs to accomplish something new;
2. Independence, that describes an individual's desire for freedom, control and flexibility in the use of time;
3. Recognition, that describes an individual's intention to reach a specific status, or to receive approval and recognition from family, friends and community;
4. Role models, that describe an individual's desire to follow family traditions or emulate the example of others;
5. Financial success that concerns an individual's intention to earn more money and achieve financial security;
6. Self-realization, which includes reasons related to the pursuit of personal goals.

Theories based on the psychological characteristics of entrepreneurship have identified the following four characteristics as key personality traits of entrepreneurs:

- Need for achievement: an individual with a high need for achievement takes responsibility for decisions, sets goals and accomplishes them through his/her effort (Brockhaus, 1982; Hansemark, 2003);
- Internal locus of control: people who have an internal locus of control perceive that events are contingent upon their own behaviour and consequently believe that they can control events through their actions (Zhao & Seibert, 2006);
- High risk-taking propensity: entrepreneurs have a strong belief in their ability to achieve goals, so the perceived possibility of failure will be relatively low and consequently the perceived risk level will be low (Chen, Greene, & Crick, 1998; Teoh & Foo, 1997);
- Capacity to build networks that could facilitate the transformation of an idea into a real plan. In this sense, networks can increase aspirations, stimulate ideas, provide practical help and give practical and financial support (Aldrich & Dubini, 1989).

These studies show that the potential entrepreneur is strongly influenced by particular psychological attitudes such as a strong desire to be independent, the search for autonomy in the workplace, the aspiration to a full exploitation of previous experiences and acquired abilities, the desire to be socially useful and to reach a better social status (Dawson, Henley, & Latreille, 2009). With regard to the latter aspect, entrepreneurship as a signal of self-sufficiency and individualism has been traditionally highly valued in the US but it is increasingly appreciated in European countries (Flash Eurobarometer, 2009; D'Adda et al., 2020).

The second strand of literature focuses its attention on the "push factors" which can be related to the founder's personal characteristics—such as age and education—his/her individual motivations towards entrepreneurship and the characteristics of innovation and entrepreneurial ecosystem of potential founders.

Autonomy or independence is one of the most cited pull factors for starting a business. On the other hand, necessity motives occur, for example, when (a threat of) unemployment forces people into self-employment: to start a new business can be related to a defensive attitude such as the uncertainty about future career perspectives or even the fear of becoming unemployed. This kind of start-up has been called "escape from unemployment" (Audretsch & Vivarelli, 1996; Deli, 2011). To sum up, the push theories assume that self-employment is largely opportunistic. Entry into self-employment is viewed as a response to the environmental circumstances faced by individuals. It would easily follow from this view that self-employment is positively associated with unemployment as it is argued that people who would otherwise prefer to work in paid employment are pushed into establishing their own business ventures because they cannot find suitable employment opportunities.

On the contrary, the pull theories assume that entrepreneurs have particular abilities and argue that self-knowledge of these particular abilities motivates them to engage in risk-taking entrepreneurial activity.

According to the results of surveys carried out by Storey (1982), the founder of a new firm is influenced by his/her own background, with particular reference to previous job experience or the personal knowledge of another entrepreneur (Reynolds, Carter, Gartner, & Greene, 2004).

2.2.2 *The Effects of Entrepreneurship on Employment and GDP Growth*

Another strand of literature focuses on the effects that entrepreneurship produces on employment and GDP growth.

Dejardin and Fritsch (2011) demonstrated that new firms may have positive effects on regional development and Fritsch and Schroeter (2010) found that these effects tend to occur within 10 years after the set up. In the medium term, new firms may induce displacement of existing firms that lead to increased productivity but also to an employment decline, while in the long-term, employment may increase due to the fact that additional competition by entries fosters the improvements on the supply side of the regional economy, enhancing competitiveness. This pattern generates a reallocation of resources within and between industries and sectors.

In this view, new firms, according to Schumpeterian ideas, may reinforce this processes by inducing displacement effects: "the fundamental impulse that sets and keeps the capitalist engine in motion comes from the newcomers' goods, the new methods of production or transportation, the new markets, the new forms of industrial organization that capitalist enterprise creates.…[This is a] process of industrial mutation - if I may use that biological term - that incessantly revolutionizes the economic structure from within, incessantly destroying the old one, incessantly creating a new one. This process of Creative Destruction is the essential fact about capitalism" (Schumpeter, 1942, p. 83).

The positive spillover generated by high levels of new firm formation has a stronger impact on the regions where such formation has occurred.

Fritsch and Mueller (2008) show that new firms represent the entry of new capacities into the market, producing indirect supply-side effects: entry or the possibility of entry forces the incumbents to behave more efficiently; there is an acceleration of structural change and an amplification of innovation with the creation of new markets; the presence of a greater variety of products and problem solutions.

The effect of start-up entries on employment change among sectors and may be negative or positive, depending on the sector and regions under consideration (van Stel & Suddle, 2008). Andersson and Noseleit (2011) shows that start-ups in high-tech services have significant negative impacts on employment change in other sectors. This negative effect for high-tech services can be explained by the fact that start-ups in this sector reinforce structural change through displacement.

Bosma, Stam, and Schutjens (2011), analysing The Netherlands, identify that the enhancing effects of productivity is verified for start-ups in the service sector but not in manufacturing.

According to Fritsch and Schroeter (2010) and Baptista and Preto (2011), the effect of new firm formation on regional employment is stronger in high-density regions than in rural ones.

Some authors investigate the relationship between GDP and entrepreneurship. According to Audretsch, Belitski, and Desai (2015), the local economic development has an impact of new business creation.

Also Baptista and Preto for Portugal (2011) show how regional conditions tend to be more relevant for start-ups in knowledge-based sectors.

In this sense, consideration of the local specific factors in the analysis of entrepreneurship is a relevant issue.

For these reasons, in the following section, I analyse the entrepreneurial dynamics in Italy and the entrepreneurial dynamics in Europe, taking into account the difference across countries.

3 Entrepreneurship Dynamics in Italy

The recent evolution of economy in industrialized countries has been accompanied by a shift of economic activity from traditional sectors to high-tech sectors, thus creating new regional agglomerations of high technology firms.

One measure of the change in economic activity is the dynamics in new firm formation, due to the fact that a relatively high regional rate of firm births indicates a process of concentration of resources within that region.

Europe and other industrialized countries have experienced considerable industrial restructuring in the last three decades, changing from traditional manufacturing industries towards new and more complex technologies such electronics, software and biotechnology, following the Industry 4.0 paradigm (Dubbini, Lepore, Micozzi, & Spigarelli, 2020). In this context, entrepreneurship and small firms play a particularly important role for two main reasons: (a) the use of new technologies has reduced the importance of scale economies in many sectors (Acs, Carlsson, & Karlsson, 1999; Dubbini et al., 2020); (b) the increasing pace of innovation and the shortening of product and technology life cycles favour new entrants and small firms, which have greater flexibility to deal with radical changes than large firms (Christensen & Rosenbloom, 1995).

The effects of new business formation amplify the regional knowledge stock and may lead to significant improvements in the competitiveness of an economy, industry or region. In this sense, firm formation is supposed to stimulate economic growth; moreover, the literature review in the previous section has shown that during the last two decades there was a relevant reversal of perspective about the role of firm formation in the development process of industrialized countries.

In Italy the debate on the role of SMEs is particularly important since the size structure of our economy, and specifically of the manufacturing industry, is "abnormally" biased towards small firms operating in traditional sectors.

Some scholars have interpreted this feature as an expression of the delay of our country in the process of industrialization, and consider it as an element of weakness and backwardness (Becattini, 1987). Others consider the prevalence of SMEs as the result of the consolidation of a production organization model based on small and medium enterprise systems (for example industrial districts or clusters of innovation) (Becattini, 1987).

Literature on small firms in Italy has focused on the characteristics of SMEs and the conditions that determine their birth and growth.

During the 80s Garofoli (1991) shows a situation of stagnations in the South area and a high dynamic in the NEC (North-East and Centre) area. Vivarelli (1994) analyses the period 1985–1990 to evaluate the dynamics of entrepreneurship in Italy and finds that the number of firms increased in this period as well as the prominence of small and medium firms. Moreover, the demographic profile of firms reflected the division of Italy into three parts (the 3 Italys) (Bagnasco, 1977). This evidence is consistent with several features of the Italian economy: productive decentralization, higher flexibility of small firms, industrial district model (Becattini, 1987).

During the 80s, there was a fall in new firm formation despite the expansive economic cycle. This occurred for several reasons. Productive decentralization due to the high cost of labour and the necessity to face a more differentiated demand fostered the creation of micro firms in the seventies. However, in the 80s the cost of labour increased and flexible technology was adopted also by large firms. Despite the growth of demand, the development of small firms decreased especially for manufacturing sectors.

To explain these Italian characteristics, Becattini (1987) proposed a model where every industry is characterized by some medium or large companies ("core") and a large number of small businesses that are subject to high "turbulence" determined by the continuous entry of new firms.

In a later work Contini and Revelli (1986) develop a model for explaining birth rates inspired by entry models. In their model the birth rate of enterprises is a linear function of entry costs, degree of industry concentration, territorial specialization, market size, growth rates of companies and risk of closure. The results of several econometric estimates show that entry costs and degree of concentration of industry have a negative influence on the entry rate. The growth rate of the sector and the territorial specialization has always the expected positive sign.

Santarelli and Sterlacchini (1993) introduce the variable "salary of employees", which is the one most used by researchers in analysing the processes of firm creation in Italy.

Foti and Vivarelli (1994), analysing the entrepreneurial rates in the period 1985–1988 in Italy, use the following independent variables: profits, salaries of employees and layoffs. The authors define the birth rate as relationship between new businesses and population (according to the self-employment approach) and find that expected profits are only one of the factors that influence business creation, taken together with the specific conditions of the labour market (i.e. rate of unemployment).

The conclusions of these analyses are not unique, as often happens for complex phenomena, such as the formation of new businesses (and entrepreneurship in general): the explanation models of this phenomenon are influenced not only by the geographical area or chosen period, but also by the manner in which the variables are defined and measured (more than that of the econometric tools used).

In this sense there is still a need to identify the determinants of formation of new businesses and the explanations of regional differences in this process.

Starting from "stylized facts", Italian birth rates were traditionally considered higher than those of other European countries; however, this is also associated with high mortality rates, especially for young business, given that the majority of new ones were very small. To the best of my knowledge, there is a lack in the literature about the phenomenon of entrepreneurship in Italy in recent years. Given the difficulties experienced by the Italian economy in adapting to the raising challenges of globalization and technological progress this seems a major research gap, due to the importance of entrepreneurship for innovation and economic growth.

Cainelli, Iacobucci, and Micozzi (2020) show that the territorial differences of entrepreneurial rates show a strong persistence over time in Italy: provinces with high entry rates in the past are most likely to have a high level of start-up activity in the future. This is true most of all for the new firms in manufacturing sectors where the factors referring to the social and economic context are important and are stable over time. The provinces of the North-Eastern and Central regions have a long tradition in manufacturing and, most of all, are characterized by the relevant presence of small firms organized in specialized clusters (industrial districts). These characteristics are responsible for the higher rates of entrepreneurial rates in manufacturing observed in these provinces. Besides the structural differences between provinces, the persistence observed in entrepreneurial rates can be explained as a result of path dependence processes in entrepreneurial dynamics. Although the entrepreneurial rate decreased in Italy in the period considered, the fall in provinces with a high level of manufacturing activities is less relevant.

3.1 The Entrepreneurial Dynamics in Italy from 2002 to 2019

As shown in the previous section, from the second half of the eighties, several research groups have investigated the phenomenon of the formation of new companies in Italy, using two different data sources: Movimprese (from the Chambers of Commerce) and INPS (National Institute for Pensions).

The Movimprese database provides the stock of registered companies, active companies, new registrations, cancellations, changes of activities, by province and sector.

Firms are classified by legal form.

The Law 580/1993 and DPR 581/1995 extended the registration for all entrepreneurs and Movimprese, after this new legislation on the registration of companies, covers the business demographic better than other databases such as INPS database.

At the same time, this source has some limitations like "spurious" births, related to registration of firms that change the legal form of a business or transfer the firm in a different province; or change the ownership structure.

According to an estimation of Garofoli (1994) for the Lombardy and Emilia-Romagna regions, these spurious births are about 25–30% of new registrations, even if we can suppose that the percentage of spurious births will not significantly change between years and provinces, so we can consider this bias a systematic bias that doesn't affect the results observed per years and province.

To define the entrepreneurial rates by provinces and by years we have to consider several approaches (labour market approach, ecological approach) (Audretsch & Fritsch, 1994a).

From a theoretical point of view, the comparison of birth rates across regions requires normalizing the numbers of new firms to a variable capturing the size of the territory.

The most appropriate denominator for the new initiatives is the total number of people in working age, in this way the estimations are not influenced by the effect of unemployment on the entrepreneurial rate.

In this analysis, I define the "rate of entrepreneurship" as the ratio between the formation of new businesses and the adult population (from 18 to 64 years), so I use the population approach.

Figure 1 shows the firm formations from 2002 to 2019 and Fig. 2 shows the entrepreneurial rate from 2002 to 2019. The data show a constant decline of entrepreneurial dynamics.

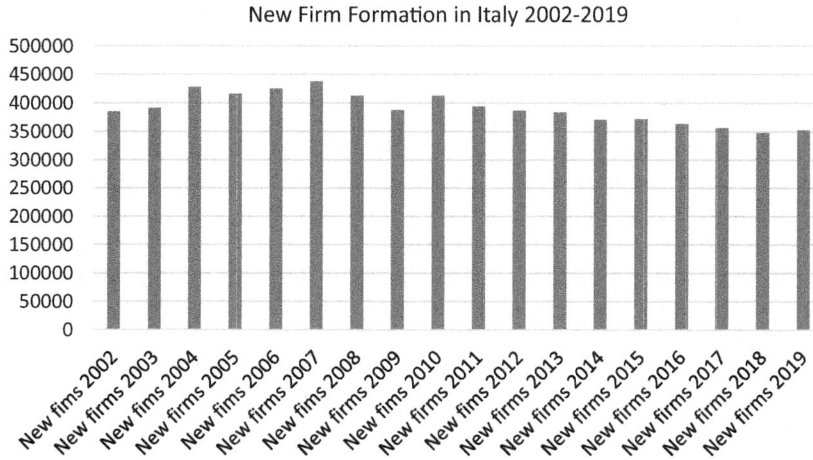

Fig. 1 New firm formation in Italy (2002–2019) (*Sources* Author's elaboration based on Movimprese database)

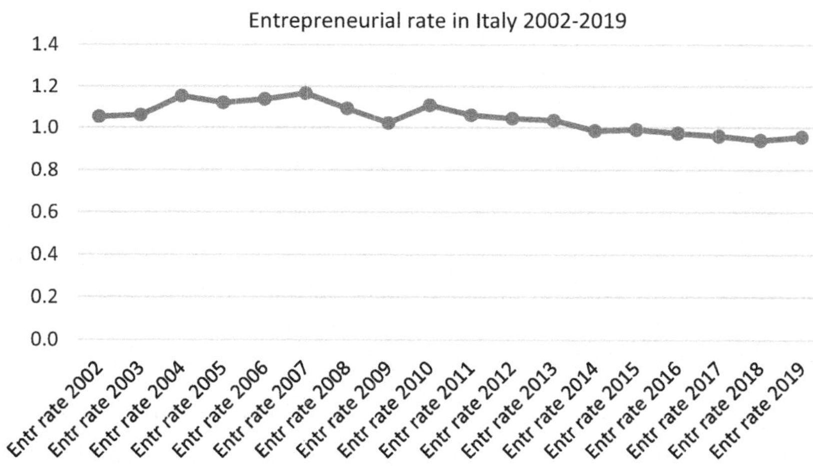

Fig. 2 Entrepreneurial rate in Italy (2002–2019) (*Sources* Author's elaboration based on Movimprese database)

3.2 *The Territorial Differences Among Provinces*

The geographical differences in the formation of new businesses is one of the aspects of this phenomenon that has attracted the attention of scholars, given the importance attributed to entrepreneurship in the development and transformation of economic systems.

The empirical literature on regional disparities in the formation of new businesses identified a large number of explanatory variables. Davidsson et al. (1994) in a study on Sweden classified these variables into four categories:

1. Micro level: variables related to potential entrepreneurs that are:
    - Socio-demographic (age structure, education, employment status)
    - Experience (occupational structure)
2. Macro level: variables related to market conditions (population density, population growth and income)
3. Variables related to availability of capital that are:
    - Private capital (income and wealth per capita)
    - Direct and indirect public support
4. Social variables linked with environment (culture of entrepreneurship, mechanisms of welfare state, etc.).

From a dynamic perspective, the explanatory factors can be classified into two categories: supply and demand side. On the demand side, the framework focuses on factors that influence the industrial structure and the diversity of consumers' preferences and habits, such as technological development, globalization and standard of living of persons. The supply side looks into various structural characteristics of the population and the way these affect the likelihood of someone becoming an entrepreneur. Examples of such factors are population growth, urbanization rate, age structure, participation of women in the labour market, income levels and unemployment rate. While the supply and demand sides refer to the macro level, the micro level integrates the decision-making process explaining how and why individuals make the choice to become an entrepreneur as opposed to other job opportunities.

Also the environment in which business is conducted plays a crucial role in fostering or weakening entrepreneurial activities both in terms of firm creation and firm growth.

From a policy point of view, these framework conditions are the aspects that define the innovation and entrepreneurial ecosystem. Issues such as the fiscal environment, labour market regulations, administrative complexities, intellectual property rights, bankruptcy law, bureaucracy, education and skill upgrading are crucial in determining the entrepreneurial dynamism of an economic context. These aspects are linked with the degree of legitimation and moral approval of entrepreneurship from a cultural point of view. The entrepreneurial culture is defined as a social context where entrepreneurial behaviour is encouraged and consists in entrepreneurial orientation of the local population and distribution of entrepreneurial characteristics among local institutions (political and educational institutions). This view claims that a higher overall level of legitimation of entrepreneurship implies more attention to entrepreneurship within the educational system, a higher social status of entrepreneurs, and also policy actions to encourage business start-ups.

Geographic factors can have a strong influence in start-up activity and they can be human capital and labour skills, unemployment rate, population density, mean establishment size, mean manufacturing wage and local taxes. Several studies found that the impact of specific geographic factors on start-up activity apparently varies considerably from industry to industry (Audretsch & Fritsch, 1999).

For example, in some industries, such as wood furniture, clothing, mechanical engineering, electrical engineering, leather and glass, the location of start-ups tends to be shaped by specific geographic factors. However, in other industries, such as mineral oil processing, aerospace, chemicals, rubber or office machines & computers, the geographic factors have little or no influence on the location of start-ups.

In this sense, the concentration of production activities is the result also of the presence of agglomeration economies. These economies are linked to three factors: (a) the local labour market; (b) the externalities linked to the offer of specialized services (c) the presence of knowledge spillovers. Agglomeration and urbanization effects were introduced by Marshall (1920) and developed by Krugman (1991). The presence of a pooled labour market for workers with industry-specific skills is more likely in agglomerations and urban areas than in rural areas. In addition, urban areas usually attract younger, better-educated adults, providing a source of entrepreneurial talents. These effects of agglomerations and urban areas are usually proxied by population density, the proportion of managers in the workforce and the proportion of graduates in the workforce.

Also Fritsch (1992) finds that there is a positive correlation between the entrepreneurial rate and the share of the regional labour force that is employed in SMEs. This finding can be interpreted considering that small firms have some kind of role as a "seedbed" for entrepreneurship. In fact, many nascent entrepreneurs had been working in small firms before they decided to start their own business and so they developed entrepreneurial qualifications in their previous experience (Storey, 1982).

Moreover, in the majority of cases, the new business is located quite close to the founder's residence, implying that the founders represent an important part of a region's endogenous economic potential.

Carloni, Ciarrocchi, and Micozzi (2020), through the use of localization software, map the position of innovative start-ups in Italy and their distance from the main research centres in the established province. According to the Knowledge Spillover Theory of Entrepreneurship (KSTE) (Audretsch & Lehmann, 2005), the analysis of data shows how innovative Italian start-ups tend to establish themselves in the immediate proximity of research centres (universities), which thanks to advanced research generate knowledge spillovers, valued on the market by entrepreneurs with high human capital able to seize the entrepreneurial opportunity that is created from these knowledge spillovers.

Ghani, Kerr, and O'Connell (2014) find strong evidence of agglomeration economies in India's manufacturing sector, emphasizing the importance of input–output relationships among firms in this sector.

Garofoli (1991) analyses the firm formation in Italy during the 80s and finds that the industrial structure and employment opportunity have an impact on the new firm formation. In his study Garofoli considers:

1. The local production structure (number of sectors, presence of industrial district, related variety).
2. The size of firms;
3. The structure of employment by categories;
4. Social structure, with specific reference to the share of independent workers, and ownership structure, with specific reference to the proportion of population that owns a house (to own a house it is

viewed as opportunity or guarantee to start a new business, thinking to the role of garage or basement where workers started an activity by themselves).

The dependent variables to which Garofoli (1994) associates these regional characteristics are:

1. New firm formation rate: number of new manufacturing firms/resident population * 1000
2. New firm formation rate: number of new manufacturing firms/active population * 1000
3. New firm formation rate: number of new manufacturing firms/manufacturing employment * 1000

The most important explanatory variables of the phenomenon are, in order: the index of production specialization, the share of independent workers in the local economy (or industry manufacturing), the percentage of employees with management and control roles and the presence of small firms.

Concerning the correlation between the regional unemployment rate and the level of new firm formation, the findings are contradictory. On the one hand, it has been well documented in the labour literature that the wage rate is negatively related to the unemployment rate. Therefore, an increase in regional unemployment should reduce the utility of wage work at the regional level and contribute to firm formation. On the other hand, Tervo and Niittykangas (1994) found evidence that regional start-up formation is negatively related to the level of unemployment, but positively related to the growth of unemployment. The former reflects a lack of business opportunities and the latter reflects a weakening of opportunities for paid employment, which pushes individuals who are unemployed to self-employment.

Another aspect concerns the demand side: the set-up of new businesses may be stimulated by prospering demand (Storey, 1982). Reynolds (1994) shows that demand growth is the most important variable explaining regional firm formation in some European countries and the US.

The market growth rate is usually measured by growth of regional per capita GDP and population, and by the rate of immigration.

Firm formation may be subject to liquidity constraints (Evans & Jovanovic, 1989), so the likelihood that a new firm will be founded could be influenced by personal or household wealth that reduces the financial barriers to firm formation.

Cainelli et al. (2020) show that Italy is characterized by large territorial differences in entrepreneurial rates. The persistence of territorial differences may depend on the differences in explanatory variables of entrepreneurial rates or on the presence of path-dependent effects. For the empirical analysis, the authors consider the creation of new firms in Italy from 2001 to 2008 at territorial level (103 provinces) and disaggregated by sector of activity. Using the adult population as normalizing variable, the entrepreneurial rate is defined as the total number of new firms in a year on the adult population at the beginning of the same year. They find a negative effect of unemployment on entrepreneurial rates that confirms the predominance of the discouraging effect of unemployment on the refugee effect. Moreover, local unemployment has a negative impact on persistence thus suggesting that the refugee effect holds only as a second-order condition.

3.3 *The Entrepreneurial Process*

In the previous section, I considered new business registrations as a proxy for entrepreneurship.

The first reason is that data on new firm registrations from public records are available for many countries.

However, researchers interested in the empirical analysis of entrepreneurial dynamics agree that new data sets, methods and definitions are needed to analyse the phenomenon properly. Shane (2012), examining the impact of the 2010 Academy of Management Review Decade Award article on the entrepreneurship field over the past ten years, sustains that entrepreneurship is not merely the formation of new firms, because this is only one institutional arrangement for the entrepreneurship phenomenon that could be defined as the process of identification, evaluation and exploitation of opportunities.

In this sense, data from sources such as Movimprese do not reflect the start-up process accurately. There are two principal reasons for this. First, entry into entrepreneurship is not always successful: only about one half of all aspiring business founders succeed in creating new organizations that appear in public records (Aldrich, 1999). This means that only those nascent entrepreneurs whose firms survive are studied, missing many interesting cases that do not succeed in completing the process of market entry. Moreover, surveys which ask entrepreneurs who start up a new business to recall the circumstances and attitudes at the inception of the venture are susceptible to hindsight bias, that refers to the incorrect reporting of information caused by memory loss and the interpretation of facts in a personal way as a consequence of events that occurred after start-up rather than before it. In this sense, hindsight bias results in a biased, or systematically distorted, recreation of the past (Fischhoff, 1975).

Another problem concerns the different measures used to study the entrepreneurial activity that prevents meaningful comparisons across countries.

All countries collect official data on entrepreneurship, however different national sources don't allow the comparison across countries, due to the fact that the data sources differ in the way they define when a nascent entrepreneur becomes a start-upper.

Moreover, given that entrepreneurial dynamics play a key role in the economic development of nations and regions, to know information about nascent entrepreneurs is important for understanding crucial aspects of the economy in a country. So, in the following section we use the database collected by the Italian team of GEM (Global entrepreneurship monitor) consortium.

4 Entrepreneurial Dynamics

Recognition of the limitations of conventional data sets stimulated a pioneering consortium of researchers, led by Paul Reynolds, to develop new databases that avoid the problems highlighted in the previous section. There are two main data sets that attempt to do this: the Panel Study of Entrepreneurial Dynamics (PSED) and the Global Entrepreneurship Monitor (GEM).

These databases allow the comparison of data sources used for the construction of entrepreneurship indicators across countries. This is a necessary condition to understand the phenomenon and evaluate the policy initiatives addressed at fostering entrepreneurial activities (Salas-Fumas & Sanchez-Asin, 2013).

The new approach proposed by GEM and PSED is that data are reflective of entrepreneurial intent and capture the spread between individuals who could potentially start a business and those who actually do so. These data represent also the potential supply of entrepreneurs, i.e. nascent entrepreneur, whereas the data on existing businesses, such as Movimprese in Italy, represent the actual rate of entrepreneurship.

Following the definition used in PSED and GEM a nascent entrepreneur is defined as a person who is now trying to start a new business, who expects to be the owner or part-owner of the new firm, who has been active in trying to start the new firm in the past 42 months, and whose start-up did not have a positive monthly cash flow that covers expenses and the owner–manager salaries for more than three months (Wennekers, van Stel, Thurik, & Reynolds, 2005).

4.1 The GEM Model

Reynolds and Curtin (2008) describes the screening process of GEM, showing that one screening item was initially used, focusing on personal efforts to pursue new firm creation. Thereafter a second item was added, asking about efforts to start a new firm as part of a job assignment. After the first survey it was discovered that many individuals who considered themselves as running a business were in the start-up phase, a third item was added to locate owner managers.

The questions in the GEM survey are:

A. Are you, alone or with others, now trying to start a new business?
B. Are you, alone or with others, currently trying to start a new business, including any form of self-employment?
C. Are you, alone or with others, currently trying to start a new business, including any form of self-employment or selling any goods or services to others?
D. Are you, alone or with others, now trying to start a new business or new venture for your employer? An effort that is part of your job assignment?
E. Are you, alone or with others, now trying to start a new business or a new venture for your employer, an effort that is part of your normal work?
F. Are you, alone or with others, currently the owner of a business you help manage, including self-employment or selling any goods or services to others?

The answers to the first four items allowed the identification of individuals who claim they are starting a new firm for themselves or their employer; expect to own all or part of the new firm; currently own and manage a firm, and; have, in the past 42 months, personally provided funds for a new business start-up. If any of these criteria applied, participants were asked follow-up questions to determine whether they were actively involved in the business, the business type, the first year receiving wages or profits, and other information on the entrepreneurship process. All of these criteria are a necessary requirement to identify nascent entrepreneurs.

Afterwards, nascent entrepreneurs are classified into a dichotomous category—necessity versus opportunity—based on the respondents' perception of the motivation that encourages the entrepreneurial initiative. Opportunity entrepreneurship represents the voluntary choice to create a new firm. On the contrary, necessity entrepreneurship occurs when an individual has no other option for employment and so decides for self-employment.

The business owners are divided into two categories based on the time since initial profits were reported. Those with profits for less than 42 months are considered new businesses; those with profits for over 42 months are considered established businesses.

The rate of individuals in the working-age population who are actively involved in business start-ups, either in the phase preceding the birth of the firm (nascent entrepreneurs), or the phase spanning 42 months after the birth of the firm (owner–managers of new firms) is defined as Total Early-Stage Entrepreneurship Activity (TEA). For the purpose of international comparisons, GEM takes the payment of any wages for more than three months to anybody (including the founders) as the birth event.

Figure 3 summarizes the entrepreneurship process and GEM's operational definitions.

The objectives of GEM are to (1) systematically assess the level of start-up activity considering the prevalence of nascent entrepreneurs and the prevalence of new or young firms that have survived the start-up phase; (2) identify how an entrepreneurial activity varies over time; (3) analyse why some countries are more entrepreneurial than others; (4) find what kind of policies enhance national entrepreneurial rates; and (5) recognize the relationship between entrepreneurship and economic growth (Reynolds et al., 2005).

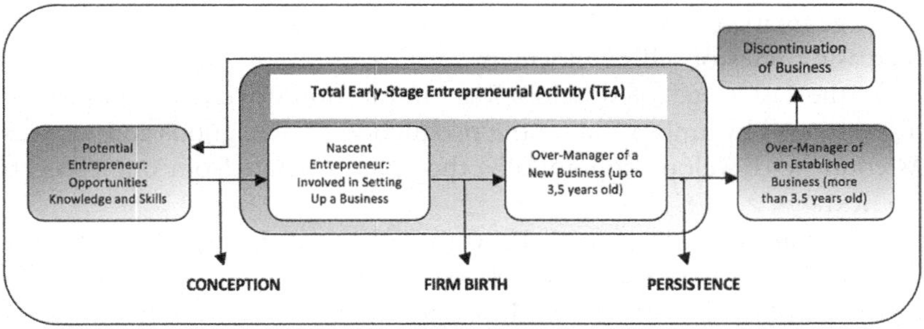

Fig. 3 The entrepreneurship process and GEM operational definitions (*Source* Gem Global Report, 2020)

Starting with just 10 developed countries in 1999, GEM has grown to include over 80 economies during the course of these 21 years.

Fifty economies participated in the GEM 2019 Adult Population Survey (APS), including 11 from the Middle East & Africa, eight from Asia & Pacific, eight from Latin America & Caribbean, and 23 from Europe & North America. The countries are grouped into three levels: factor-driven, efficiency-driven and innovation-driven. According to the World Economic Forum's classification, the factor-driven phase is dominated by subsistence agriculture and extraction businesses, with a heavy reliance on labour and natural resources. In the efficiency-driven phase, further development is accompanied by industrialization and an increased reliance on economies of scale, with capital-intensive large organizations being more dominant. As development advances into the innovation-driven phase, businesses are more knowledge intensive, and the service sector expands.

Porter, Sachs, and McArthu (2002) define the three groups of countries: countries in the factor-driven stage compete with low-cost production and low value-added products. In this first stage nascent entrepreneurs start-up small business in manufacturing sectors or service firms. Almost all economies experience this stage.

The second stage is the efficiency-driven stage and countries must increase their efficiency in production and the workforce show a higher human capital than workforce of factor-driven countries. The sectors that characterized this second stage of competitiveness are the manufacturing sector or basic services and the competition is on efficient production on large markets. The efficiency-driven stage is characterized also by decreasing rates of self-employment.

At the last stage of development, innovation-driven, economies are characterized by innovation on the production of new goods and services. As countries develop economically, they tend to shift from one phase to the next.

Each country collects from 1000 to 27000 surveys per year. Figure 4 shows TEA rates across the sample of 50 economies analysed in the last Global Report (2019) of GEM, organized into the four geographical areas and exhibited within each from lowest to highest TEA rate.

This figure facilitates benchmarking among economies in the same area. Italy shows the lowest TEA index.

If we consider the entrepreneurial rate in each country, the 2019 results show that the rate of established business ownership declines with greater economic wealth (Fig. 5).

The data show that the share of nascent entrepreneurs differs widely between countries.

Several authors investigated what makes a country more or less entrepreneurial. Van Stel, Carree, and Thurik (2005), using data for 36 countries participating in the Global Entrepreneurship Monitor in 2002,

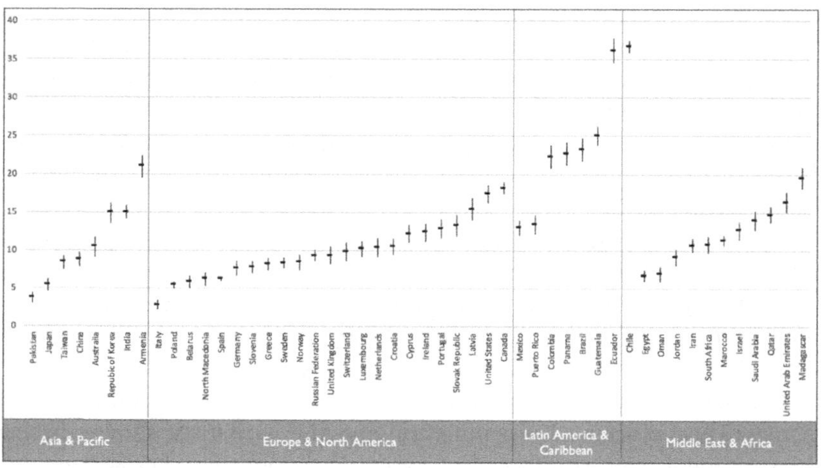

Fig. 4 Total early-stage entrepreneurial activity (TEA) for 50 economies in 2019, by area (*Source* Bosma et al., 2020)

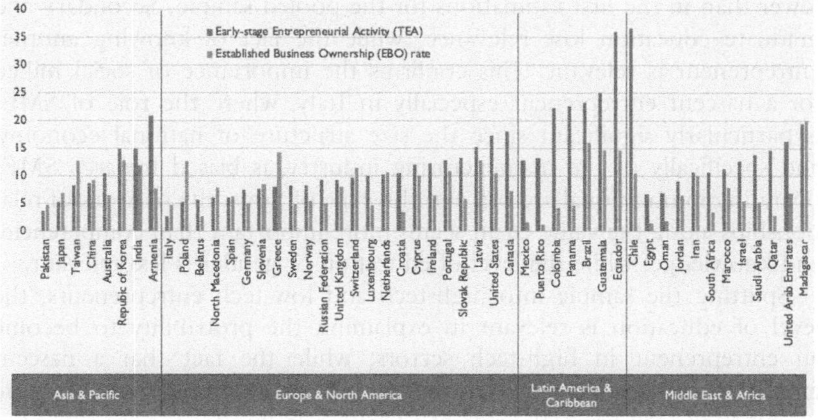

Fig. 5 Established entrepreneurial activity for 50 economies in 2019, by area (*Source* Bosma et al., 2020)

find a U-shaped nexus between nascent entrepreneurship and the level of economic development of a country, using per capita GDP as an indicator and considering the effect of the innovative capacity of countries.

Also Acs, Armington, and Zhang (2006) show that differences in the dynamics of entrepreneurship across countries depend on institutional context and level of economic development.

Micozzi (2013) analyses the factors affecting the probability to become a nascent entrepreneur in Italy comparing with a pool of nine European countries. According to GEM, Italy showed the lowest index of entrepreneurial rate in the global ranking and the lowest share of new high-tech firms in comparison with other EU countries. The importance of fostering the creation of new firms derives from the current scenario of deep and significant changes to the labour market, characterized by exponential growth of youth unemployment. In these conditions, young people encounter few opportunities in the labour market and self-employment could represent a survival strategy. Micozzi (2013) finds that gender, the level of education and the fact that the person knows someone who started a firm, influence the probability to become an entrepreneur but with different results for pooled sample (considering nine European countries) and Italian sample. The regressions for Italy show that gender influences the probability to start a new business but the influence is lower than in the first estimations for the pooled sample. Secondary and graduate education lose relevance, while the fact of knowing another entrepreneur is relevant. This confirms the importance of social milieu for a nascent entrepreneur especially in Italy, where the role of SMEs is particularly significant since the size structure of national economy, and specifically of the manufacturing industry, is biased towards SMEs operating in traditional sectors. For this type of firms, the network of relationships along the value chain seems more important than competencies and knowledge, while the level of education or gender is less relevant.

Splitting the sample into high-tech and low-tech entrepreneurs, the level of education is relevant in explaining the probability to become an entrepreneur in high-tech sectors, while the fact that a nascent entrepreneur knows another entrepreneur loses significance. In the case of new high-tech firms, the role of education is emphasized as well as the gender gap (Micozzi, 2013).

The survey of Eurobarometer (Flash Eurobarometer, 2009) in the EU, EFTA countries, Croatia, Turkey, US, Japan, South Korea and China on entrepreneurship in the EU focused on two questions in particular:

- Why do so few Europeans set up their own business?
- Why are so few European businesses growing?

The question of Eurobarometer can be rearticulated in:

- What national characteristics are associated with differences in the prevalence of business creation?
- Which factors are more associated with participation in business creation, national characteristics or personal attributes and local context?
- Which specific variables, reflecting national characteristics, local context, and personal attributes, have the greatest association with individual participation in business creation?

In the following, I try to answer these questions, using data from the Gem APS of Italy.

4.2 From a Nascent Entrepreneur to an Established Business

Reynolds (2010) summarizes graphically (Fig. 6) the major initial stages of the business life course, analysed above, and the factors that may affect these different stages; they are classified into three broad categories or levels of analysis: the national context, personal context and personal attributes.

People may decide to start businesses when they recognize specific entrepreneurial opportunities. The quantity and quality of opportunities that individuals perceive, and their beliefs about their capabilities (self-efficacy), may be affected by various conditions in their environment: for example, economic growth (level of GDP per capital), culture and education (number of graduates). Different demographic groups may make distinct judgments about opportunities and capabilities; and this is affected by historical, socio-economic or cultural factors.

Bosma et al. (2020) observe a distinction in the recognition of opportunities between some northern and southern regions: Nordic countries have the highest opportunity perception, while economies in Southern Europe (as Italy) tend towards a low opportunity perception. Self-efficacy shows opposite evidence. Nordic countries had below average belief about

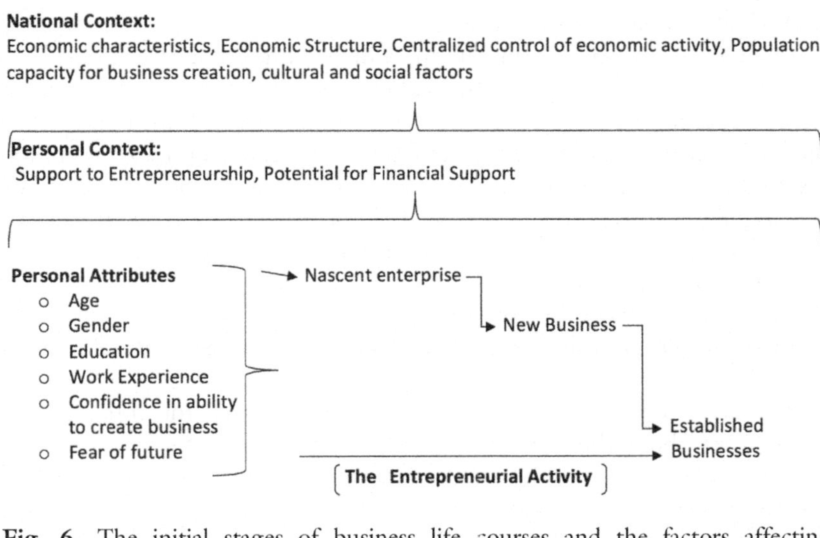

Fig. 6 The initial stages of business life courses and the factors affecting participation in the firm life course (*Source* Reynolds, 2010)

capabilities, while the Southern European countries, with the exception of Italy, were under the average level on this attitude. Analyses of GEM data have suggested very strong effects of self-reported confidence in having the relevant skills for running one's own business (Arenius & Minniti, 2005). Self-efficacy (Bandura, 1982) refers to the extent to which a person believes that he/she can organize and effectively implement actions to produce given achievements.

Concerning the risk of failure, even if the expected returns from entrepreneurship can be considerably higher than the best alternative, the perceived risks of starting a business may nonetheless discourage some individuals. Risk-taking propensity can therefore play a significant role in the transition from potential entrepreneurship (nascent entrepreneur) to an effective business start-up.

Characteristics such as age, gender or ethnicity can influence fear of failure. Young people may not have families and loans to support so they have less to lose in a certain sense. Immigrants may have fewer options for generating income. The institutional environment can also impact this; for instance, bankruptcy legislation may deter those aspiring to become entrepreneurs.

While perceptions about opportunities and capabilities show significant differences among the groups of countries, fear of failure shows less distinction among these groups.

Of course, a local context in which entrepreneurial culture is widespread fosters or prevents the willingness to become an entrepreneur. An entrepreneurial culture may be reinforced by perceptions that to start up a new firm is an attractive activity. Media can emphasize common ideas about entrepreneurs: for example, magazines or television shows can highlight entrepreneurs, showing the achievements of such individuals and spread the imagine of entrepreneurs as heroes, talking about their stories of success.

Policymakers may even take specific actions to highlight entrepreneurs and their importance for economy and society and shape cultural perceptions.

The last GEM survey (Bosma et al., 2020) shows the difference in perceptions about the attractiveness of entrepreneurship as a career, the status of entrepreneurs and media attention towards entrepreneurship: Japan has the lowest proportion of adults agreeing that they see good opportunities to start a business, followed by the Russian Federation and Belarus. At the other end of the scale, almost nine out of 10 adults in Poland see good opportunities in starting a business, followed by India, Sweden, China and three Middle Eastern countries: Saudi Arabia, Qatar and Egypt. Even when individuals have favourable perceptions of entrepreneurship, they may nonetheless have few intentions to start businesses. This is the case for many European countries. Although attitudes and perceptions about entrepreneurship can be high, people can show low intentions for starting businesses. A variety of national characteristics could underlay this phenomenon. For example, governments that put particular attention on welfare states, as in Italy, may reduce incentives for entrepreneurship.

4.3 Necessity vs. Opportunity

All people considered active in the GEM survey are asked if they are involved in entrepreneurship by taking advantage of a business opportunity (opportunity nascent entrepreneur), or due to the fact that they have no better options for work (necessity nascent entrepreneur), or a combination of motives. Opportunity entrepreneurship is linked to pull motivation, while necessity entrepreneurship is often related to push motivation.

Global assessments indicate that two-thirds of entrepreneurs self-classify as opportunity motivated while one-third self-classify as necessity motivated (Reynolds et al., 2004).

Opportunity entrepreneurship has a strong correlation with high technology and high growth-oriented firms. On the other hand, necessity entrepreneurship is significantly correlated with subsequent increases in economic growth. The fact that necessity versus opportunity (or push versus pull) entrepreneurship is largely determined by the level of economic development can explain why Uganda has a TEA higher than Italy: many people in Uganda start an entrepreneurial career for lack of other opportunities.

Gross domestic product (GDP) growth has no significant impact on necessity entrepreneurship but a positive impact on opportunity entrepreneurship (van Stel et al., 2007).

In developed economies, we would expect that entrepreneurial activity be positively related to economic growth due to the fact that people have more possibility to shift from wage work to entrepreneurial career in response to the perceptions of opportunities within the market.

Also the economic and entrepreneurial context in terms of hostility, munificence, and dynamism will impact on entrepreneurial motivation and influence the process of opportunity recognition (D'Adda et al., 2020).

4.4 *Main Evidence for Italy from GEM 2019*

TEA in Italy showed a considerable decrease between 2007 and 2010, the year in which the TEA dropped to its minimum value in the period considered (2.3%). Subsequently there is a progressive, albeit not constant recovery, until 2015, the year in which it returned to pre-crisis values, with a TEA of around 5%.

In the following years, a slow decline in the indicator is observed, up to the sharp drop observed in 2019, the year in which the indicator value is around 3%.

The component of entrepreneurship by necessity is very limited in Italy, recording fluctuations in the period considered between 0.5 and 1%. In 2019 this component marks the lowest value, around zero.

In general, in advanced countries, of which Italy is a part, the percentage of entrepreneurship by opportunity is much higher than that by necessity and the latter is almost never the determining component of the performance of TEA. However, in Italy the necessity component is among the lowest ever, similar to that observed in Sweden and Switzerland. The low percentage of entrepreneurship by necessity is probably due to the good level of economic security and access to essential services ensured by our welfare system. At the same time, this system seems to be poorly incentivized towards entrepreneurial activity.

If from the temporal trend we pass to the consideration of the absolute value of the TEA indicator, Italy in 2019 is confirmed at the bottom of world ranking, with values much lower than those of European countries and very distant from those observed in Canada and US.

The weighted average of TEA for the 15 EU countries included in the 2019 survey is 6.8% (the unweighted average is 9.6%); therefore, more than double the value recorded in Italy (2.8%).

The decision to start a new business is the product of individual attitudes, perceptions and intentions, within an ambient, social and cultural context that can encourage or limit this decision. Whatever the context, in order to be successful, the entrepreneur must have relationships with a wide range of stakeholders, including investors, employees, suppliers and customers, as well as the support of family and friends. These different individual and contextual factors are investigated by the GEM survey through several questions; for example, asking the interviewee if she/he knows someone who has started a new business, or if she/he believes that there are good opportunities to start a new business in her/his local area or how easy she/he thinks it is to start a business in her/his own country. Knowing someone who has started a business can increase awareness for this choice, and facilitate the assessment of the costs and benefits associated with it. Knowing an entrepreneur means having a "role model" and a greater possibility of developing useful relationships for entrepreneurial activity. The importance of these aspects is evident from the greater entrepreneurial propensity shown by people whose parents or family members are involved in, or have been involved in, an entrepreneurial activity.

The perception of good opportunities to start a business can indicate the existence of an innovation potential, but it also depends on the ability to recognize these opportunities. Finally, the judgement on the ease or not in starting a business reflects the way in which people perceive the environment as enabling or binding for entrepreneurial activity.

In Italy, as can be observed in other countries, there is a high discrepancy between the entrepreneurial intention, i.e. the declared interest in future entrepreneurial activity, and the entrepreneurial propensity, i.e. the effective implementation of this intention.

If we consider the data relating to 2018 (which confirm the trend of previous years), it emerges that the entrepreneurial intention expressed by Italians is similar to the values observed in the EU average; on the contrary, the Italian value is decidedly lower than the average when we consider the actual involvement in the business activity.

The level of entrepreneurial intention is an important indicator of the consideration that the population has of entrepreneurship. The indicators of perception of the social value of entrepreneurship are: entrepreneurship as a good career opportunity, the social status of successful entrepreneurs and the attention paid by the media to entrepreneurial activities. These indicators in Italy are in line with or above the European average. Entrepreneurship is perceived positively in our country and this explains the high share of the population that expresses its intention to start an entrepreneurial activity. The problem seems to emerge in the transition from intention to implementation.

The GEM survey on the adult population allows us to investigate the subjective factors that may explain the discrepancy between entrepreneurial intention and actual activation. These factors include the personal knowledge of entrepreneurs, the perception of the presence of entrepreneurial opportunities, the perception of the adequacy of one's skills and the fear of failing. In all these elements, our country presents a worse situation than the European average.

Among Italians, the perception of the opportunity to start a business is lower than the European average and the percentage of those who believe they have the necessary skills to start a business is significantly lower. These factors also condition the fear of failure which is higher in our country than the EU average (D'Adda et al., 2020).

Next to the subjective aspects, the contextual ones must be considered. One of the main contextual factors is certainly the shortcomings of the school system and tertiary education. Italy is among the European countries with the lowest percentage of graduates out of the adult population. The level of education affects the ability to perceive opportunities in the environmental context, especially for knowledge-based initiatives and in the perception of the skills necessary for starting a business. Worsening this picture is the limited presence of entrepreneurial training programmes in school and tertiary education cycles. This is in stark contrast to the recommendations in this regard from the EU Commission.

As a consequence, Italy shows the lowest entrepreneurial rate in high-tech sectors.

The competitiveness of Italy in the global economy depends extensively on scientific, technological and innovation-based assets. Unfortunately, several studies show that in Italy and Europe the flow of the results of public research towards industrial applications is not without obstacles. The "European Paradox" is well-known: Europe suffers from a gap between high levels of scientific performance and lower levels of contributions to economic competitiveness, especially with regard to high-tech sectors and new innovative start-ups (Dosi, Llerena, & Sylos, 2006; Rodríguez-Navarro & Narin, 2018). As a consequence, the attention on the role of Universities in research that generate spillover of knowledge which entrepreneurs can valorize into the market is necessary (Audretsch & Lehmann, 2017). According to Braunerhjelm, Acs, Audretsch, and Carlsson (2009), entrepreneurs are the missing link between knowledge and the capability to valorize this knowledge on the market.

Since the mid-1990s, universities worldwide have been progressively involved in the valorization of their research results, which includes both commercialization and other activities generating economic and social impact. As a consequence, the phenomenon of entrepreneurial universities has received considerable attention due to the fact that the entrepreneurial orientation of universities can provide valuable contributions to knowledge-based economy (Bathelt, Kogler, & Munro, 2010; Budyldina, 2018; Jain, George, & Maltarich, 2009; Lazzeroni & Piccaluga, 2003).

For this reason, in the following chapter, I analyse the phenomenon of academic entrepreneurship.

Bibliography

Acs, Z. J., Armington, C., & Zhang, T. (2006). The determinants of new-firm survival across regional economies. *Papers in Regional Science, 86*(3), 39.

Acs, Z. J., & Audretsch, D. B. (1989). Entrepreneurial strategy and the presence of small firms. *Small Business Economics, 1,* 193–213.

Acs, Z. J., Carlsson, B., & Karlsson, C. (1999). *Entrepreneurship, small and medium-sized enterprises and the macroeconomy.* Cambridge: Cambridge University Press.

Aldrich, H. (1999). *Organizations evolving.* London: Sage.

Aldrich, H., & Dubini, P. (1989). Le reti e i processi di sviluppo delle imprese. *Economia e Politica Industriale, 64,* 363–375.

Amit, R., Glosten, L., & Muller, E. (1993). Challenges to theory development in entrepreneurship research. *Journal of Management Studies, 30*(5), 815–834.

Andersson, M., & Noseleit, F. (2011). Start-ups and employment dynamics within and across sectors. *Small Business Economics, 36,* 461–483.

Arenius, P., & Minniti, M. (2005). Perceptual variables and nascent entrepreneurship. *Small Business Economics, 24*(3), 233–247.

Audretsch, D. B. (1995). Firm profitability, growth, and innovation. *Review of Industrial Organization, 10*(5), 579–588.

Audretsch, D. B., Belitski, M., & Desai, S. (2015). Entrepreneurship and economic development in cities. *The Annals of Regional Science, 55*(1), 33–60.

Audretsch, D. B., & Fritsch, M. (1994a). On the measurement of entry rates. *Empirica, 21,* 105–113.

Audretsch, D. B., & Fritsch, M. (1994b). The geography of firm births in Germany. *Regional Studies, 28*(4), 359–365.

Audretsch, D. B., & Fritsch, M. (1999). The industry component of regional new firm formation processes. *Journal of Industrial Organization, 15,* 239–252.

Audretsch, D. B., & Lehmann, E. E. (2005). Does the knowledge spillover theory of entrepreneurship hold for regions? *Research Policy, 34*(8), 1191–1202.

Audretsch, D. B., & Lehmann, E. E. (2017). The knowledge spillover theory of entrepreneurship and the strategic management of places. In G. Ahmetoglu, T. Chamorro-Premuzic, B. Klinger, & T. Karcisky (Eds.), *Wiley handbook of entrepreneurship* (pp. 1–51). London: Wiley.

Audretsch, D. B., & Vivarelli, M. (1996). Firms size and R&D spillovers: Evidence from Italy. *Small Business Economics, 8*(3), 225–237.

Bagnasco, A. (1977). *Tre Italie. La problematica territoriale nello sviluppo italiano*. Bologna: IL Mulino.

Bandura, A. (1982). Self-efficacy mechanism in human agency. *American Psychologist, 37*(2), 122–147.

Baptista, R., & Preto, T. M. (2011). New firm formation and employment growth: Regional and business dynamics. *Small Business Economics, 36,* 419–442.

Bathelt, H., Kogler, D., & Munro, A. (2010). A knowledge-based typology of university spin-offs in the context of regional economic development. *Technovation, 30*(9–10), 519–557.

Becattini, G. (1987). *Mercato e forze locali: il distretto industriale*. Bologna: Il Mulino.

Bewley, T. (2002). Interviews as a valid empirical tool in economics. *Journal of Socioeconomics, 31*(4), 343–353.

Birch, D. L. (1987). *Job creation in America: How our smallest companies put the most people to work*. New York: Macmillan and Free Press.

Bosma, N., Hill, S., Ionescu-Somers, A., Kelley, D., Levie, J., & Tarnawa, A. (2020). *Global entrepreneurship monitor. 2019/2020 global report*. London.

Bosma, N., Stam, E., & Schutjens, V. (2011). Creative destruction and regional productivity growth: Evidence from the Dutch manufacturing and services industries. *Small Business Economics, 36,* 401–418.

Braunerhjelm, P., Acs, Z. J., Audretsch, D. B., & Carlsson, B. (2009). The missing link: Knowledge diffusion and entrepreneurship in endogenous growth. *Small Business Economics, 34*(2), 105–125.

Brockhaus, R. H. (1982). The psychology of the entrepreneur. In C. A. Kent, D. L. Sexton, & K. H. Vesper (Eds.), *Encyclopedia of entrepreneurship* (pp. 39–71). Englewood Cliffs: Prentice Hall.

Budyldina, N. (2018). Entrepreneurial universities and regional contribution. *International Entrepreneurship and Management Journal, 14*(2), 265–277.

Cainelli, G., Iacobucci, D., & Micozzi, A. (2020). Discouraged entrepreneurs and persistence in local entrepreneurship. The Italian case, 2001–2008. *L'Industria*, 1–16.

Carloni, M., Ciarrocchi, A., & Micozzi, A. (2020). La vicinanza all'Università? Un'opportunità. Le scelte di localizzazione delle start-up innovative italiane. *L'Industria, XLI*(4), 81–102.

Carter, N. M., Gartner, W. B., Shaver, K. G., & Gatewood, E. J. (2003). The career reasons of nascent entrepreneurs. *Journal of Business Venturing, 18*(1), 13–39.

Chen, C. C., Greene, P. G., & Crick, A. (1998). Does entrepreneurial self-efficacy distinguish entrepreneurs from managers? *Journal of Business Venturing, 13*(4), 295–316.

Christensen, C. M., & Rosenbloom, R. S. (1995). Explaining the attacker's advantage: Technological paradigms, organizational dynamics, and the value network. *Research Policy, 24*(2), 233–257.

Contini, B., & Revelli, R. (1986). Natalità e mortalità delle imprese italiane: risultati preliminari e nuove prospettive di ricerca. *L'Industria, 7*(2), 195–231.

Cromie, S., & Hayes, J. (1988). Towards a typology of female entrepreneurs. *Sociological Review, 36*(1), 87–113.

D'Adda, D., Iacobucci, D., Micozzi, A., & Micozzi, F. (2020). *Rapporto Gem Italia 2019–2020*. Fabriano.

Davidsson, P., & Henrekson, M. (2002). Determinants of the prevalance of start-ups and high-growth firms. *Small Business Economics, 19*(2), 81–104.

Davidsson, P., Lindmark, L., Olofsson, C., & Business, J. I. (1994). New Pirm Formation and Regional Development in Sweden. *Regional Studies, 28*(4), 395–410.

Dawson, C. J., Henley, A., & Latreille, P. L. (2009). *Why do individuals choose self-employment?* (IZA Discussion Paper No. 3974).

Dejardin, M., & Fritsch, M. (2011). Entrepreneurial dynamics and regional growth. *Small Business Economics, 36*, 377–382.

Deli, F. (2011). Opportunity and necessity entrepreneurship: Local unemployment and the small firm effect. *Journal of Management Policy and Practice, 12*, 38–57.

Dosi, G., Llerena, P., & Sylos, M. L. (2006). The relationships between science, technologies and their industrial exploitation: An illustration through the myths and realities of the so-called 'European paradox'. *Research Policy, 35*, 1450–1464.

Dubbini, S., Lepore, D., Micozzi, A., & Spigarelli, F. (2020). Il modello marchigiano e industria 4.0: potenzialità e criticità. *L'Industria*. Published online.

Dyer, J. W. G. (1994). Toward a theory of entrepreneurial careers. *Entrepreneurship: Theory & Practice, 19*, 7–21.

European Commission. (2010). *European innovation scoreboard 2009*. PRO INNO Europe.

European Commission. (2011). *Horizon 2020—The framework programme for research and innovation.*

Evans, D. S., & Jovanovic, B. (1989). An estimated model of entrepreneurial choice under liquidity constraints. *Journal of Political Economy, 97*(4), 808–827.

Fischhoff, B. (1975). Hindsight is not equal to foresight: The effect of outcome knowledge on judgment under uncertainty. *Journal of Experimental Psychology: Human Perception and Performance, 1*(3), 288–299.

Flash Eurobarometer. (2009). *Entrepreneurship in the EU and beyond.*

Foti, A., & Vivarelli, M. (1994). An econometric test of the self-employment model: The case of Italy. *Small Business Economics, 6*(2), 81–93.

Freytag, A., & Thurik, R. (2007). Entrepreneurship and its determinants in a cross-country setting. *Journal of Evolutionary Economics, 17*(2), 117–131.

Fritsch, M. (1992). Regional differences in new firm formation: Evidence from West Germany. *Regional Studies, 26*(3), 233–241.

Fritsch, M., & Mueller, P. (2008). The effect of new business formation on regional development over time: The case of Germany. *Small Business Economics, 30,* 15–29.

Fritsch, M., & Schroeter, A. (2010). Why does the effect of new business formation differ across regions? *Small Business Economics, 36*(4), 383–400.

Garofoli, G. (1991). The Italian model of spatial development in the 1970s and 1980s. In G. Benko & M. Dunford (Eds.), *Industrial change and regional development: The transformation of new industrial spaces* (pp. 85–101). London: Belhaven.

Garofoli, G. (1994). La formazione di nuove imprese in Italia: analisi dei differenziali territoriali. In Istituto Guglielmo Tagliacarne (Ed.), *Formazione di nuove imprese: un'analisi comparata a livello internazionale* (pp. 62–99). Milano: Franco Angeli.

Ghani, E., Kerr, W. R., & O'Connell, S. (2014). Spatial determinants of entrepreneurship in India. *Regional Studies, 48*(6), 1071–1089.

Hansemark, O. (2003). Need for achievement, locus of control and the prediction of business start-ups: A longitudinal study. *Journal of Economic Psychology, 24*(3), 301–319.

Jain, S., George, G., & Maltarich, M. (2009). Academics or entrepreneurs? Investigating role identity modification of university scientists involved in commercialization activity. *Research Policy, 38*(6), 922–935.

Kelley, D. J., Bosma, N., & Amorós, J. E. (2011). *Global Entrepreneurship Monitor (GEM) 2010 Annual Global Report. Global Entrepreneurship Research Association GERA*. Global Entrepreneurship Research Association.

Kihlstrom, R. E., & Laffont, J.-J. (1979). A general equilibrium entrepreneurial theory of firm formation based on risk aversion. *Journal of Political Economy, 87*(4), 719–748.

Kirzner, I. M. (1982). The theory of entrepreneurship in economic growth. In D. L. Sexton, C. A. Kent, & K. H. Vesper (Eds.), *Encyclopedia of entrepreneurship* (pp. 272–276). Englewood Cliffs, NJ: Prentice Hall.

Kirzner, I. M. (1985). *Discovery and the capitalist process*. Chicago: University of Chicago Press.

Knight, F. H. (1921). *Risk, uncertainty and profit*. Boston and New York: Houghton Mifflin.

Krugman, P. (1991). Increasing returns and economic geography. *Journal of Political Economy, 99*(3), 483–499.

Lazear, E. P. (2000). The power of incentives. *The American Economic Review, 90*(2), 410–414. Retrieved from http://www.jstor.org/stable/117260.

Lazear, E. P. (2005). Entrepreneurship. *Journal of Labor Economics, 23,* 649–680.

Lazzeroni, M., & Piccaluga, A. (2003). Towards the entrepreneurial university. *Local Economy, 18*(1), 38–48.

Leibenstein, H. (1968, May). Entrepreneurship and development. *American Economic Review, 58*(2), 72–83.

Locke, E. A. (1976). The nature and causes of job satisfaction. In M. D. Dunnette (Ed.), *Handbook of industrial and organizational psychology* (Vol. 1, pp. 1297–1349). Rand McNally. Retrieved from http://www.getcited.org/pub/103369589.

Lucas, R. E. (1978). Asset prices in an exchange economy. *Econometrica, 46*(6), 1429–1445. https://doi.org/10.2307/1913837.

Marshall, A. (1920). *Principles of economics*. London: Macmillan.

Micozzi, A. (2013). Factors affecting the entrepreneurial dynamics in Italy: A comparison across European countries. *Economia Marche Journal of Applied Economics, XXXII*(1), 129–145.

OECD. (2003). *Turning science into business. Patenting and licensing at public research organizations*. Paris: OECD.

OECD. (2010). *SME's, entrepreneurship and Innovation.*

OECD/EUROPEAN UNION. (2019). *Supporting entrepreneurship and innovation in higher education in Italy.*

Porter, M., Sachs, J., & McArthur, J. (2002). Executive summary: Competitiveness and stages of economic development. In M. Porter, J. Sachs, P. K. Cornelius, J. W. McArthur, & K. Schwab (Eds.), *The global competitiveness report 2001–2002* (pp. 16–25). New York: Oxford University Press.

Reynolds, P. D. (1994). Autonomous firm dynamics and economic growth in the United States, 1986–1990. *Regional Studies, 28*(4), 429–442. https://doi.org/10.1080/00343409412331348376.

Reynolds, P. D. (2010). New firm creation: A global assessment of national, contextual, and individual factors. *ReVision, 6*(5–6), 315–496.

Reynolds, P. D., Carter, N., Gartner, W., & Greene, P. (2004). The prevalence of nascent entrepreneurs in the United States: Evidence from the panel study of entrepreneurial dynamics. *Small Business Economics, 23*(4), 263–284.

Reynolds, P. D., & Curtin, R. T. (2008). Business creation in the United States: Panel study of entrepreneurial dynamics II initial assessment. *Foundations and Trends in Entrepreneurship, 4*(3), 155–307.

Reynolds, P., Bosma, N., Autio, E., Hunt, S., De Bono, N., Servais, I., Lopez-Garcia, P., & Chin, N. (2005). Global Entrepreneurship Monitor: Data Collection Design and Implementation 1998–2003. *Small Business Economics, 24*(3), 205–231.

Rodríguez-Navarro, A., & Narin, F. (2018). European paradox or delusion—Are European science and economy outdated? *Science and Public Policy, 45*(1), 14–23.

Salas-Fumas, V., & Sanchez-Asin, J. J. (2013). Entrepreneurial dynamics of the self-employed and of firms: A comparison of determinants using Spanish data. *International Entrepreneurship and Management Journal, 9,* 417–446.

Santarelli, E., & Sterlacchini, A. (1993). Profili e determinanti settoriali della formazione di nuove imprese nell'industria italiana. *Rivista Di Politica Economica, 83*(5), 33–68.

Schjoedt, L., & Shaver, K. G. (2007). Deciding on an entrepreneurial career: A test of the pull and push hypotheses using the panel study of entrepreneurial dynamics data. *Entrepreneurship: Theory & Practice, 31*(5), 733–752.

Schumpeter, J. A. (1942). *Capitalism, socialism, and democracy.* New York: Harper & Brothers.

Schumpeter, J. A. (1943). *Capitalism, socialism, and democracy.* London: G. Allen & Unwin.

Schumpeter, J. A. (2000). Entrepreneurship as innovation. In R. Swedberg (Ed.), *Entrepreneurship the social science view* (pp. 51–75). Oxford: Oxford University Press.

Shane, S. (2012). Reflections on the 2010 AMR decadee award: Delivering on the promise of entrepreneurship as a fiel of research. *The Academy of Management Review, 37*(1), 10–20.

Storey, D. J. (1982). *Entrepreneurship and the new firm.* Londra: Croom-Helm.

Teoh, H. Y., & Foo, S. L. (1997). Moderating effects of tolerance for ambiguity and risk taking propensity on the role conflict-perceived performance relationship: Evidence from Singaporean entrepreneurs. *Journal of Business Venturing, 12,* 67–81.

Tervo, H., & Niittykangas, H. (1994). The impact of unemployment on new firm formation in Finland. *International Small Business Journal, 13*(1), 38–53.

Van Stel, A., Carree, M., & Thurik, R. (2005). The effect of entrepreneurial activity on national economic growth. *Small Business Economics, 24*(3), 311–321.

Van Stel, A., Storey, D. J., & Thurik, A. R. (2007). The effect of business regulations on nascent and young business entrepreneurship. *Small Business Economics, 28*(2–3), 171–186.

van Stel, A. J., & Suddle, K. (2008). The impact of new firm births and job creation: Is there an Upas tree effect. *Small Business Economics, 30,* 31–47.

Vivarelli, M. (1994). *La nascita delle imprese in Italia. Teorie e verifiche empiriche.* Milano: EGEA.

Wagner, J. (2004). *Are young and small firms hothouses for nascent entrepreneurs? Evidence from German micro data* (IZA Discussion Paper No. 989).

Welter, F., & Lasch, F. (2008). Entrepreneurship research in Europe: Taking stock and looking forward. *Entrepreneurship: Theory and Practice, 32*(2), 241–248.

Wennekers, S., & Thurik, R. (1999). Linking entrepreneurship and economic growth. *Small Business Economics, 13,* 27–55.

Wennekers, S., van Stel, A., Thurik, R., & Reynolds, P. (2005). Nascent entrepreneurship and the level of economic development. *Small Business Economics, 24*(3), 293–309.

Zhao, H., & Seibert, S. E. (2006). The big five personality dimensions and entrepreneurial status: A meta-analytical review. *The Journal of Applied Psychology, 91*(2), 259–271.

CHAPTER 2

Academic Entrepreneurship

Abstract The second chapter analyzes the phenomenon of academic entrepreneurship that could be defined as the direct involvement of academicians that valorize into market the results of academic research. The commercialization of scientific and technological knowledge represents a fuel for fostering the regional economic growth, and a way to valorize research results into market is the creation of new firms: the academic spin-offs.

Keywords Academic entrepreneurship · Academic spin-offs · Knowledge-based firms · Technology transfer

1 Introduction

In the first chapter, I examined how entrepreneurship is linked with growth and development of economic systems and how globalization and technology can have an impact on this relationship. Economic activities based on knowledge provide a strong base for the comparative advantage of high-cost economies as they cannot easily be imitated or transferred to other regions. A new source of competitiveness for innovation-driven countries therefore lies in a knowledge-driven economy: the ability of countries to reach and maintain economic growth based on technology

A. Micozzi, *The Entrepreneurial Dynamics in Italy*,
https://doi.org/10.1007/978-3-030-55183-4_2

and knowledge is a fundamental issue in recent approaches to economic growth theory (Romer, 1990).

As competitiveness in the knowledge economy is based on innovation it is important for countries to foster the creation of new knowledge and new product development (Audretsch, 2012).

Three strands of the literature can be distinguished in the study of links between knowledge and growth. The first strand links research and development (R&D) to output: R&D is an important prerequisite for innovation and innovation consequently increases productivity.

The second strand links human capital to growth: human capital relates to the quality of labour and can be seen as the tacit knowledge that is created by education and experience.

The third strand links entrepreneurship capital to output. Entrepreneurship capital is the capacity of economic agents to generate new firms (Audretsch et al., 2006).

The rise of the knowledge economy changes the coordination and cooperation among the main actors involved in the economy (government, knowledge institutions and the business community), particularly in relation to the diffusion and exploitation of knowledge so a tighter integration is needed between industry, universities, public research facilities and government policy in the areas of science and technology (Carayannis & Campbell, 2010).

We are witnessing a "radical, irreversible, worldwide transformation in the way that science is organised and performed" (Ziman, 1994, p. 7).

In present times, the university has three missions: research and teaching—two activities that produce externalities in the form of human capital and knowledge spillover—and technology transfer (TT). Shifting towards knowledge-based economies, there is an increasing demand for basic knowledge and highly skilled people. In this respect, universities play a critical role in the supply side contributing to the productivity growth and expansion of industry and services.

Since the mid-1990s, universities and research organizations have been increasingly involved in commercializing research results. This trend was formalized in a range of legislation promoting technology transfer as the third mission of universities.

If we accept that knowledge-based economies are innovation-driven, universities should be crucial stakeholders in the innovation process to drive economic development, especially in a country such as Italy characterized by a lack of research-based innovations and by European Paradox. In this sense, universities can represent a key resource for high-tech firms, especially in the early stages of product development, by providing firms with innovative technical solutions or devices, or by the involvement in applied research. As a result, governments and public opinion have placed more emphasis on the third mission of university, also by commercializing their own academic inventions.

TT was fostered by a legislation that encourages universities to register patents and licenses. This new approach started in the US with the Bayh-Dole Act of 1980 and continued in several European countries, with the abolition of the "professor's privilege", which recognized academicians' full rights to their innovations (the professor's privilege remains confirmed in Italy). The increase of government funding for research projects in technology areas, is also the result of a new attitude to foster academics to valorize the results of their research on the market through the foundation of new firms (academic spin-offs) and management of intellectual property rights.

In this change of perspective, industry started to increase its attention towards university research, shifting from a vertical model of R&D to an open innovation strategy, based upon the exploitation of external knowledge spillover generated by university research.

The Open Innovation perspective (Chesbrough, 2003) offers a framework to discuss the links between actors involved in innovation process, due to the fact that it consists in "the use of purposive inflows and outflows of knowledge to accelerate internal innovation, and expand the markets for external use of innovation, respectively. Open innovation is a paradigm that assumes that firms can and should use external ideas as well as internal ideas, and internal and external paths to market, as they look to advance their technology" (Chesbrough, 2003, p. 1).

A large part of open innovation literature takes the perspective of the firm in relations with universities and several approaches to hypothesizing these interactions have been developed. The most important is the triple helix model and the idea of the entrepreneurial university (Etzkowitz & Leydesdorff, 2000). The triple helix model has been used as a way of understanding the interconnection of three major components of national innovation systems: university, industry and government. In the triple helix model, interaction among these actors is identified as being the key to innovation and resultant economic growth.

The effectiveness of the relations between university and industry depends on several factors such as the sector of activity and its stage of evolution, firm absorptive capacities, institutional autonomy, the reputation of the university and its response to political support at international, national and regional levels.

Starting from these premises, in this chapter I investigate the particular kind of knowledge-based entrepreneurship, the academic entrepreneurship.

The first step is defining the concept of entrepreneurial university, academic entrepreneur and university technology transfer, using a taxonomy developed from the literature.

2 Key Concepts in Academic Entrepreneurship

2.1 Entrepreneurial Universities

The entrepreneurial university emerged first in the US, followed by the UK and subsequently throughout Europe and the rest of the world.

Public research organizations, and in particular universities, have become increasingly entrepreneurial, embracing a mandate for the realization of commercial value from research, and searching for new organizational configurations that bring a closer association of scientific research and innovation (Rothaermel et al., 2007), in response to the growth of an entrepreneurial academic paradigm that stresses the concept of knowledge capitalization (Etzkowitz, Webster, Gebhardt, & Terra, 2000).

Since the early 1990s, universities have been called to play a more central role in supporting economic growth. Indeed, the EU policy on science and technology has used incentives to promote knowledge transfer from university towards industry.

At the same time, universities themselves have become willing actors in the exploitation of research results to improve the means for generating revenue and adapt to a more competitive environment. As a consequence, there has been a growth in the variety and volume of collaboration between university and industry, and an increased emphasis on using commercialization of intellectual property at the institutional level (Lockett & Wright, 2005).

Increasingly engaging in interactions with industry, the core of the university system expands to include activities outside the ivory tower with the purpose of transforming inventions into innovations for the benefits of society.

Rothaermel et al. (2007) identify important questions on entrepreneurial university research, such as: how can universities be more successful in entrepreneurial activities? why are some universities more entrepreneurial than others? how do entrepreneurial universities relate to entities outside the ivory tower? and what are the barriers to universities becoming more entrepreneurial?

In the following section, I try to collect the answers of literature.

2.2 *Academic Entrepreneurship*

The concept of the "academic entrepreneur" was born in the American system of research organization (Budyldina, 2018; Meoli & Vismara, 2016; Siegel & Wright, 2015). Indeed, in US universities, academics traditionally act like entrepreneurs due to the fact that they are involved not only in research but also in several entrepreneurial activities. The "academic entrepreneur" is a university scientist, such as a professor or a Ph.D. student or a postdoc researcher, who sets up a firm in order to commercialize the results of her/his research. The qualifying adjective "academic" stresses the fact that the innovations introduced by the entrepreneur originate from the research she/he conducted as part of her/his job (Foray & Lissoni, 2010).

The organization of scientific research, especially in experimental and applied sciences, are necessarily entrepreneurial: researchers at the head of large laboratories perform several activities typical of an entrepreneur, such as setting up and managing complex organizations and teams, and providing them with adequate funding and human capital.

Etzkowitz's (1983) in his essay on "Entrepreneurial scientists and entrepreneurial universities in American academic science", one of the best-known papers on entrepreneurship in academy, describes this pattern as one of diffusion of "quasi-firms" (laboratories and research groups), since their existence depends on the ability of attracting and recruiting talented and skilled people and of gaining funding.

2.3 *University Technology Transfer*

University technology transfer is a step-by-step process of commercializing university-developed technology and invention whose success is dependent on the role played by a researcher who becomes an academic entrepreneur when she/he engages in the commercialization of the results of her/his research, largely by patenting and/or setting up a new firm (Bradley, Hayter, & Link, 2013).

The literature investigates the benefits of university technology transfer: it includes a more rapid technological diffusion to the public enhancing local and regional economic development, it is a potential source of university revenue, it could have a positive effect on the curriculum of academics involved in these activities and the orientation of universities towards the third mission may attract students, faculty and additional industrial research support. On the other hand, potential risk exists such as negative impact on culture of open science affecting the type of research questions addressed, possible reduction of the quantity and quality of basic research due to the fact that academics spend less time on teaching and working on scientific papers.

The technology transfer activities would have an impact mainly in three ways: by influencing the productivity of scientific research, by restricting the academic freedom or by reorienting academic research towards more applied projects.

In this regard, Lissoni (2010) identifies a dilemma: entrepreneurial activities of scientists create decline of scientific productivity. The empirical literature suggests that scientists who engage in patenting do not seem to suffer a decline of scientific productivity. On the contrary, some evidence exists on the relevance of this dilemma: "Do commercial interests discourage some scientists to publish the research results in order to advance knowledge?" (Mathieu, 2011).

For the central administration of universities there is a problem of balance among the three missions: university can choose to encourage the technological commercialization or to create a structure that is neutral towards those who choose to be directly involved in commercialization of results of research and towards those who choose to not be.

In an entrepreneurial university, technology commercialization of research results can take place through various mechanisms that are:

- formal mechanisms (patenting, university licensing, strategic alliance through formal and informal research partnerships or joint ventures, and the creation of university spin-outs or spin-offs);
- informal mechanisms (knowledge transfer, consulting and joint publications with industry scientists).

On the basis of these types of academic entrepreneurship, Oliver (2004) identifies three types of academic entrepreneurs: those who manage research teams in conducting big projects; academic scientists who use their knowledge to set up or collaborate with commercial firms, and finally those scientists who realize the commercial value of their work through patents and licenses or through the creation of a new firm.

The rise in entrepreneurial activities of universities generates a need to better understand how it can be measured. Several options are proposed by scholars: most measures of entrepreneurial activities are focused on commercial output, including university licensing (number of licenses, licensing revenue), equity positions, number of invention disclosures, number of sponsored researches, royalties, number of spin-offs and patents (number of patents, efficiency in generating new patents) (Rothaermel et al., 2007).

In the following, the different types of technology transfer are described.

Publication

The publication of articles in academic journals represents the most important way in which research discoveries conducted at universities are made public (Rogers et al., 2001).

Publication in prestigious journals brings status to the researcher and the university. Moreover, it forms an important method to assess the quality of the academic research. Although they are very important in this respect, publications do not provide an effective means of technology transfer due to the fact that journal articles are usually written for fellow scientists rather than for potential users of the technology (Clarysse, Wright, Lockett, Mustar, & Knockaert, 2007).

Licensing

The practice of licensing has traditionally been the most popular mechanism of university technology transfer due to the fact it is a formal transfer of knowledge from universities to the commercial sector (Siegel, Waldman, & Link, 1999).

Recently, Martelli, Micozzi, Iacobucci, and Piccaluga (2019) demonstrate how the increase of employees in TTO increases the number of patent applications, showing the importance of human resources in fostering technology transfer mechanisms.

University spin-offs

Entrepreneurial spin-offs form one of the most direct ways in which technology and new knowledge created at university are adopted within a new firm. Spin-offs are therefore an important method to bring innovations, technologies and new products to the market, making use of opportunities that otherwise would have been left unexploited or undeveloped (Shane, 2002).

In the following, I try to demonstrate that these knowledge-based firms created through the spin-off process can be a source of new jobs, accelerate regional economic growth, create a new sector or renovate an existing one, and increase a region's competitiveness. In addition to these benefits the spin-off process provides an option in the careers of researchers, enabling them to actively develop the technical application of their research. Equity participation in a spin-off will provide the scientist with enough incentive to put a lot of effort into this commercialization.

Spin-offs are something more complex than a license. At the invention stage, universities have an important role in the generation of new scientific and technological knowledge that has traditionally been codified in the form of a patent, which can be developed through formal transfer of the technology as license to an established company. Alternatively, the transfer of technology can happen through the creation of a company in which the researcher becomes part of the entrepreneurial team (Wright, Clarysse, Lockett, & Knockaert, 2008).

Contract research

Typically, contract research between a university researcher and a firm is referred to as applied research. From a commercial and economical point of view, it means to exploit the tacit knowledge held by the scientists in the university and this generates revenues for the research team in the forms of research funds. For firms, contract research can represent a way of acquiring knowledge that can generate additional profit and knowledge enhancement of its R&D workforce (Shane, 2002).

Consulting

Consulting typically involves interaction between the academicians and industry in order to find a solution to a technical problem (Denis & Lomas, 2003).

Graduate and researcher mobility

An important way in which knowledge is transferred from university into industry is through the skills and experience embedded in graduates and researchers (Argote & Ingram, 2000). This knowledge may be tacit in the form of the knowledge and skills that the graduate has within her/his mind, rather than a codified formal transfer. Graduates from universities might embody the absorptive capacity that industry needs to have to identify opportunities for interactions with universities. Concerning the innovation and entrepreneurial ecosystem, graduates may be an important source of local knowledge transfer due to the fact that they will often remain in their local area (Acosta, Coronado, & Flores, 2011; Åstebroa, Bazzaziana, & Braguinskyb, 2012).

2.3.1 A Comparison of Type of Technology Transfer Mechanism

University patents, spin-off company creation, consulting and joint research agreements are often addressed as separate, alternative transfer mechanisms. In this sense, commercializing the results of university research may require a mix of all those instruments.

Barbieri, Rubini, Pollio, and Micozzi (2018) show that the effectiveness of a technology transfer tool can be better assessed by considering the possible substitution effects with other channels of knowledge transfer. They verify whether creating academic spin-offs has an impact on the overall patenting and publication performance and results suggest that there is a negative effect on the overall publishing performance, while the patenting activity does not change significantly. Regarding co-publications, the results of empirical analysis in Italy confirm the existence of a substitution effect between spin-offs and co-publication with firms, while the authors observe an increase in the case of co-patenting. Ferri and Fiorentino (2019) show how the number of patents has positive effects on ASOs' growth performance.

Concerning the motivation that foster academicians to valorize the results of their research within the market, Stephan and Levin, (1996) show that individual scientists, rather than pursuing patenting only for personal enrichment, may disclose their research results because they hope to access further funds for their on-going research.

Moreover, the decision on what is the best way to valorize the research results (by patent licensing or by a start-up) depends also on the technological regime and on the appropriability of the innovation. In low-appropriability patent regimes, licensing may be hard and innovations may not be commercialized because of a lack of incentives.

Shane (2004) found that the probability of patenting an invention was higher in strong appropriability regimes. In a related study he also found that the spin-off rate increased with the novelty and importance of the technology behind it.

Lowe (2001), analysing the technology transfer activities at the University of California, found that patents with a stronger scientific base and a higher degree of tacit knowledge were more likely to be licensed to their inventors, and the creation of spin-offs is needed when the knowledge of a researcher is highly uncodified (for example when the academic invention is disclosed at a proof-of-concept stage) (Shane, 2004).

The age and position of academicians can have an impact on the way in which researchers exploit their knowledge: younger scientists may be more willing to increase their scientific reputation through publications (Audretsch & Stephan, 1999).

However, other studies suggest that the founding of spin-offs may be an appealing option for younger researchers, such as fresh Ph.D. graduates and research assistants, whose career perspectives are limited but wish to continue to do research in close contact with their university (Iacobucci, Iacopini, Micozzi, & Orsini, 2011).

Another factor affecting the choice between licensing or spinning out concerns the intellectual eminence of the academics within the university.

Di Gregorio and Shane (2003) suggest that top universities will always look to spin-off creation.

Also the characteristics of TTO have a role in deciding whether to license or set up a company. While patenting requires larger structures with greater availability of resources, smaller universities are better suited to the implementation of forms of technology transfer characterized by consulting activities.

Academic institutions have to identify a model of TT consistent with their structural features, giving to TTO the mission, and the resources, to improve the outcomes in TT activities at local level.

In terms of financial benefits of technology transfer, it is relevant to evaluate who gets them (university, academics, firms).

In both cases (technology transfer and financial benefits) it is also relevant to evaluate the geographical span in which the benefits are obtained, that could be local, regional or national.

Table 1 shows an evaluation of geographical impact of technology transfer activities proposed by Iacobucci and Micozzi (2015).

The choice of what mechanism of technology transfer is used, depends on several factors and generates different benefits.

Iacobucci and Micozzi (2015) proposed a scheme that shows the potential benefits of spin-offs activity, comparing them with the other forms of technology transfer (Table 2).

Table 1 Geographical impact of technology transfer activities

	Local (NUTS3)	*Regional (NUTS2)*	*National/ Global*
Patenting and Licensing			**
Contract research and consulting	**	***	*
Spin-offs	***	*	

* low impact
** medium impact
*** high impact

Table 2 Pecuniary beneficiaries of technology transfer activity

	Contract research and consulting	*Patenting and licensing*	*Spin-offs*
University	share in external contracts	Fees	dividends and capital gains (when the university has a share in the spin-off)
Faculty	direct remuneration	Fees	Remunerations; dividends and capital gains
Former students and researchers			Salaries; dividends and capital gains
Firms			dividends and capital gains

In terms of financial benefits, the most important way of commercializing university research, is through contract research. Most of these benefits are appropriated directly by the academicians involved in the research and consulting activity. However, in Italy a significant share is retained by the university to cover general expenses and to contribute to the research infrastructure.

In the case of patents issued as a result of publicly funded research, the financial benefits go to the university and to the inventors, depending on who is the owner of the patent. In recent years there has been an increase in IP management by Italian universities (Ramaciotti & Daniele, 2018).

However, several studies demonstrate that even in universities that manage a large portfolio of patents the revenue form fees barely cover the expenses.

This means that patents and licenses do not make a major difference in terms of technology transfer and certainly not in terms of regional development. Universities either lose money on their patents or they make money with one patent to pay off deficits on the other ones.

The advantage of the licensing system over most other transfer methods is that both the scientist and the university are able to profit from the technology. Despite these advantages, there are several general disadvantages to licensing for both the licenser and the licensee. The new technology may not be easily patented or managed under a license agreement. Licensing a technology only transfers codified knowledge to the licensee.

Moreover, the commercial value of this knowledge is not known in advance so that the university may not be able to capture the full value of its technology through a licensing agreement (Lockett, Wright, & Franklin, 2003).

To avoid this problem, several other ways of transferring knowledge could be adopted by academic researchers. Often neglected, but perhaps more important in terms of potential revenues is knowledge transfer through contract research and consulting activities. If universities are to develop close links with industry to generate research income, they have to build areas of expertise that firms will want to access.

From the university point of view, spin-offs are not likely to be a major source of income, as compared with licensing or other technology transfer activities, and neither is significant relative to other sources of income, but they are the most important in terms of potentiality of impact on local economy. This is the reason why, in the following, I concentrate my attention on this most promising way to transfer research results to the market place.

3 Academic Entrepreneurship and Spin-Offs

3.1 Definition of Academic Spin-Offs

There is no uniform definition of the phenomenon of academic spin-offs, given the distinctive circumstances in which these knowledge-based firms are set up.

In this book, Academic Spin-Offs (ASO) are defined as "companies which evolve from universities through commercialization of intellectual property and transfer of technology developed within academic institutions" (Djokovic & Souitaris, 2008, p. 225).

In my research, I posit a transfer of technology from a university organization as a conditio sine qua non for defining a company as an academic spin-off.

Compared to other ways of transferring research results analysed, a spin-off is characterized by the following: (a) the start-up of a new company, (b) the transfer to that company of specific technological knowledge developed in universities, (c) the involvement of staff from the research institute in the ownership and management of the new initiative (O'Shea et al., 2007).

In most advanced industrial countries, the phenomenon became significant in the '80s. In the US the significant increase in licensing activities and the setting up of spin-offs by universities can be considered the result of the general growth in importance of scientific knowledge in productive activities and a progressive stance towards the university having a more active role in the economic development of the territory (Etzkowitz et al., 2000).

Many European countries, especially those in Northern Europe, have followed the trend observed in the US, albeit with some lag. European universities tried and followed the US experience during the last thirty years and this has stimulated the attention of several authors who have investigated the creation and development of spin-offs in Europe. In the majority of European countries, bringing academic research closer to business and society also became a central issue and it is somewhat at the crossroads of two major trends, R&D and Innovation policies for SMEs on the one hand and University/industry relations and transfer policies on the other, because academic spin-offs represent at the same time both one kind of innovative SMEs and one kind of mechanism of technology transfer.

As a result, over the last decades the attention paid to the spin-off phenomenon by both academic institutions and policymakers has increased considerably even in Italy (Poma & Ramaciotti, 2008). Universities have begun to play an increasingly active role in promoting and supporting spin-offs, seeing them as an opportunity to pursue several objectives: (a) develop an effective way to exploit research results; (b) contribute to production diversification and the development of the geographical areas where they are set up, (c) provide a possible source of employment for their researchers. The policymaker's attention to spin-off is justified by the need to promote the commercial fallout of investment in basic and applied research and the need to promote the development of knowledge-based entrepreneurship, which is increasingly regarded as fundamental for territorial competitiveness (Iacobucci and Micozzi, 2015; Iacobucci et al., 2011).

The relevance of academic spin-offs has initially contributed to very optimistic perceptions about their growth potentials (Heirman & Clarysse, 2004), on the basis of the highly visible success stories (the so-called 'gazelles') in the early- and mid-Nineties and the success of a few hi-tech clusters.

Several researchers later expressed their doubts about the real extent of rapid growth potentials of all academic spin-offs: several empirical studies showed that the vast majority of spin-off companies start (Chiesa & Piccaluga, 2000; Jacobsson & Rickne, 2004; Yli-Renko, Autio, & Sapienza, 2001) small and remain small, reflecting founder aspirations and commitment, managerial capabilities and resources employed in the firm.

Leitch and Harrison (2010), analysing the spin-offs in Northern Ireland, suggested that the prominence given to spin-offs in the analysis of technology transfer is inappropriate. If we look at the atypical experience in ecosystems such as Silicon Valley or the Route 128 area (Bonte, Falck, & Heblich, 2009; Nicolaou & Birley, 2003), we can affirm that the impact of technology transfer on local economy is huge. Despite this, the spin-off process in other US or EU contexts is very different from that in more developed high-tech entrepreneurial ecosystems such as Boston or Silicon Valley.

So, after several years of spin-off euphoria, some studies have started to look critically at the outputs of entrepreneurial activities of universities.

In spite of these critics, the creation of university spin-offs still represents a potentially important innovation mechanism. Therefore, it seems necessary to foster the design of policies that focus on the quality of spin-offs instead of the quantity (Clarysse & Moray, 2004).

After twenty years of experience of spin-off promotion by universities and local institutions in Italy, there is a need to assess the effective role played by these firms in an advanced economy, evaluating the impact of spin-offs on university technology transfer and local economies.

3.2 The Level of Analysis

Up to now, the empirical analyses of the phenomenon of academic entrepreneurship has focused on several aspects, analysing the characteristics of spin-offs and their growth (Iacobucci et al., 2011), the difference between those universities that have been most active in the creation of spin-offs and those that have been least active (Lockett et al., 2003), the factors that foster the creation (Iacobucci et al., 2011; Lockett & Wright, 2005), the beneficial impact on the growth of other local high-tech start-ups when these are able to detect, absorb and use this knowledge (Colombo & Piva, 2008).

Djokovic and Souitaris identify different levels of analysis for the spin-off phenomenon (Djokovic & Souitaris, 2008):

- Macro: governmental and industrial support mechanisms in the start-up process and the technology that are ready for commercialization. The tendency for an invention to be exploited through firm creation varies with the attributes of the technology regime (the age of the technical field, the tendency of the market towards segmentation and the possibility to patent the invention);
- Meso: university support mechanisms (incubators and Technology Transfer Offices), and the effectiveness of creation of a new firm such as a university technology transfer mechanism;
- Micro: characteristics of academic spin-offs, process of growth, determinants of growth, team of founders and networks with university and industry.

3.2.1 The Role of University in Fostering Academic Spin-Offs

The first theme analysed by scholars revolves around the role of the university in fostering academic entrepreneurship.

Universities can choose different policies to regulate the phenomenon and this determines different attitudes towards surrogate entrepreneurs, different methods of technology transfer, concerning equity investments and intellectual property protection, and different models of technology transfer, that could be proactive, planned or spontaneous (Lockett et al., 2003), All of these aspects play a role in contributing to or inhibiting university spin-off activities. Several authors focus on the faculty aspects, including their location, roles in the new ventures, personality, expectations, quality, experience and timing of inventions (Chiesa & Piccaluga, 2000; Clarysse & Moray, 2004; Di Gregorio & Shane 2003; Johansson et al., 2005; Leitch & Harrison, 2005; Lockett et al., 2003).

The role of the university in determining the creation and success of spin-offs concerns several themes: intellectual property, networking activities of university spin-offs, resources, and overall university involvement. University policies on intellectual property strategy, such as the encouragement of equity investments, are associated with a higher number of university spin-offs (Di Gregorio & Shane, 2003; Lockett et al., 2003). University investments in external intellectual property protection is another factor that appears to contribute to the success of spin-offs (Lockett & Wright, 2005).

Empirical evidence suggests that European universities perform less successfully than the US universities in TT especially if we consider the transfer of new knowledge from the university to the regional economy through ASOs (Franzoni & Lissoni, 2009). Several factors influence the differences between the US and Europe. Thinking about the status of researchers: university faculty members in the US are university employees whereas in Europe they are civil servants or state employees (Franzoni & Lissoni 2009) with an effect on the salary. In Europe there isn't a system to consider productivity differences that determine differences in salaries (Bonaccorsi & Daraio, 2005). Moreover, in the US there is high competition among universities for employing start scientists due to the fact that high performance researchers can attract additional public funding for the universities. Moreover, in the US the sources for research come from the government but also from foundations, Venture Capital (VC) or Business Angels. This allows a concentration of funds which is not possible in Europe where private donations are very low and the market of VC is still in an infant stage.

Effective transfer of knowledge from the university to an economic context may require intermediaries to build relationships with firms.

The distance between universities and firms in terms of language, physical distance and culture increases the importance and the complexity of these actors (Kostova & Roth, 2003).

They could be internal to the university (e.g. TTOs, incubators), or external to university (e.g. surrogate entrepreneurs, venture capital firms, science park and development agencies).

Technology Transfer Offices (TTOs) aim at fostering the commercialization and valorization of research results with a different role in different TT mechanisms (Cesaroni & Piccaluga, 2015).

According to some authors (Lockett & Wright, 2005; Smilor & Matthews, 2004; Vohara et al., 2004), a properly organized and staffed TTO can increase the productivity of university technology transfer activities (Berbegal-Mirabent, Ribeiro-Soriano, & Sánchez García, 2015).

3.2.2 Differences Across Countries

Another theme in the literature stream is concerned with the difference between countries in fostering and supporting academic spin-offs. Some countries are better at creating spin-offs than others; and in turn some universities are more entrepreneurial than others in fostering the creation of new firms in specific sectors.

Numerous explanations for these disparities have been given (Lawton Smith & Ho, 2006).

First, national governments have an impact on spin-off activity because they determine the degree to which universities have the autonomy to make their own rules regarding the technology transfer activities. The UK government, for example, provides financial and political incentives to encourage entrepreneurship and R&D tax incentives.

With respect to university autonomy, in Sweden, Italy and Finland, for example, universities do not own their staff's patent while in contrast in the UK, since 1985, the professor privilege has been abolished. In France it was only in 1999 that academic spin-offs became possible after the passing of Allegre's Law, although the national laboratories had long been able to do so.

The UK has placed the universities at the heart of policies aimed at the creation of spin-offs, which is not the case in other countries. Policy is at the university level, leading to the creation of diverse structures to support the third mission of universities and pressure at a political level led to a strong growth during the 1990s in the number and variety of linkages between university and industry. In France, the creation of new ventures by academics is considered as part of a technological entrepreneurship policy to foster the development of new high technology ventures. The European institutional context is heterogeneous across countries, which have differing traditions of policy development regarding innovation and technology transfer, so, it is not obvious that similar policies that have been successful elsewhere can feasibly be adopted in different European countries (Mustar & Wright, 2010).

The second explanation for disparities among countries and universities is that the reputation and research eminence of individual universities are strongly associated with the rate of spin-offs (Blanchflower, Oswald, & Stutzer, 2001).

Third, institutional factors identified as influencing the rate of spin-off activity include the culture of the university, its attitude towards spin-offs and the competence of the technology transfer offices (Lockett et al., 2003).

3.2.3 Type of Academic Spin-Offs

Another explanation for the different performances shown by spin-offs revolves around the fact that the distribution of spin-offs across industry sectors is highly uneven and spin-offs are diverse in their activities (Druilhe & Garnsey, 2004).

Studies also show that sector is strongly associated with spin-off activity and the impact at employment level tends to be local as most spin-offs, according to the knowledge spillover theory of entrepreneurship, stay within the same geographical area as the institution from which they originated (Shane, 2004).

Another stream of literature analyses the different kind of spin-offs. Druilhe and Garnsey (2004) identify five categories of academic spin-offs. Based on their business activities and resource necessities, spin-offs are categorized as "consultancy", "intellectual property licensing", "software", "product" and "infrastructure creation". The study shows how the business models of new ventures are modified as entrepreneurs improve their knowledge of resources and opportunities.

Heirman and Clarysse (2004) developed a taxonomy of spin-off firms: (1) VC-backed spin-offs, which are the few spin-offs that start with VC funds; (2) prospectors, which are the spin-offs that start with low clarity of the product market; (3) product spin-offs, which have a product ready to market and with a potential international market; (4) transitional spin-offs, which initially valorize the knowledge on the market through consulting and develop their product in a second phase.

Lazzeri and Piccaluga (2012) identify five clusters of spin-offs on the basis of the business model adopted.

Specifically, in Italy they show that 10.5% of academic spin-offs are technology gem, with a business model oriented to ideas of market and technology, to be appealing for big companies that could think about a strategy of M&A.

Spin-offs supported by university (17.4%) that show a strong link with parent university and have an ownership structure made up of industrial companies, have a big portfolio of licenses and adopt a business model oriented to sell product/service in the national and global market.

Spin-offs with serial entrepreneurs (23.4%) where promoters have previous business experiences in creation of high-tech firms. They offer hi-tech know-how supported by a big portfolio of licenses.

The market-ready spin-offs (18.8%) are companies with products or services ready to be commercialized. The business model aims to improve the market share and, frequently, there are in the ownership structure, promoters with previous experience in the productive functions.

Another stream of literature analyses the process of spin-off formation and defines the critical steps that an academic entrepreneur encounters.

Lockett and Wright (2005) summarize the key process issues with respect to overcoming the organizational knowledge gaps that new ventures encounter as opportunity recognition, the decision to commercialize, the choice between licensing and spin-off, and the time period over which TTOs are involved in spin-offs to help the new firms in accessing resources and knowledge.

The phases of growth are: (1) research phase; (2) opportunity framing phase; (3) pre-organization phase; (4) re-orientation stage; and finally (5) sustainable returns phase.

Vohora et al. (2004) argue that while the different stages are important it is the difficulties in moving from stage to stage that create critical junctures, which are the key challenges that an academic spin-off faces during its development. Four key critical junctures that spin-off companies need to overcome if they are to succeed are: (1) opportunity recognition, (2) entrepreneurial commitment by a venture champion, (3) attaining credibility in the business environment and (4) achieving sustainable returns within their respective markets.

An essential prerequisite for valorizing the research results into the market is that the researchers involved in research and technology transfer recognize the commercial value of the research and see an entrepreneurial opportunity to exploit this knowledge. Moreover, one or more individuals need to be willing and capable to exploit these commercial opportunities and make the start-up a success.

There are two approaches to entrepreneurship associated with the formation of spin-off companies from universities (Radosevich, 1995): the inventor-entrepreneur approach, that is the approach concerning the academic entrepreneur, and the approach that uses surrogate entrepreneurs to commercialize university knowledge. Academic entrepreneurship ensures a fundamental understanding of the company's core technology within the management of the start-up. However, even if academics are aware of the commercial opportunity that has arisen from their research, this is by no means a guarantee that they will pursue it. Researchers often experiment the lack of incentive to start a spin-off or the lack of commercial and managerial skills. These indicate that a strategy focused on academic entrepreneurship might require substantial support infrastructure from technology transfer offices and incubation centres to aid the start-up and progress of these entrepreneurial companies (Radosevich, 1995).

If the academic inventor does not possess the right entrepreneurial skills, so-called surrogate entrepreneurs need to be obtained (Ben-Hafaïedh, Micozzi, & Pattitoni, 2018; Lockett et al., 2003).

Surrogate entrepreneurship involves an external individual or organization assuming the role of entrepreneur while the academic originator maintains a position in the university (Lockett et al., 2003). With skills gained from previous entrepreneurial experience, surrogate entrepreneurs often possess the business skills and business network that the academic entrepreneur lacks.

Another important issue for nascent ventures is to gain sufficient credibility to access and acquire key resources (tangible and intangible) (Vohora et al., 2004).

To sum up, different competencies are required to start up an academic spin-off: the competency to discover opportunities, then, a leveraging competency is needed to develop the new venture and finally, a championing competency and networking competency that are needed to attract persons and institutions for growth (Rasmussen, Mosey, & Wright, 2011).

For knowledge-based firms, it is unlikely that one academic entrepreneur possesses all the competencies necessary to gain credibility for the new venture (Roberts, 1991). For this reason, ASOs are often started up by teams and internal and external actors (i.e. TTO or surrogate entrepreneurs) with different competencies connect the academic and commercial context (Clarysse & Moray, 2004; Vanaelst et al., 2006).

3.2.4 Factors Affecting the Decisions of Scientists to Become Entrepreneurs

Another stream of literature analyses the factors that influence the likelihood that a scientist becomes an entrepreneur (Franzoni & Lissoni, 2009).

Empirical studies examine the propensity of academicians to create spin-offs using characteristics of the researchers (Roberts, 1991), their entrepreneurial behaviour and characteristics of their research projects and research findings (Shane, 2001) and the attributes of academic researchers that influence the identification and exploitation of entrepreneurial opportunities (D'Este, Mahdi, & Neely, 2010).

In the case of spin-offs the commercialization activity is not limited to identifying a discovery with commercial potential, but concerns the activities for bringing it to the market.

Setting up business plans to do actions in order to explore the market potential of the discovery. These activities include the design of a business plan, finding venture capital and managing the tangible and intangible resources.

Mustar (1997) provides a detailed illustration of the complexity of setting up a hi-tech spin-off, indicating that success in such ventures requires a combination of the skills of researchers, relationship with clients during the early stage of product/technology design and the capacity to search for public and private funding sources to support the firm in its initial phase and the subsequent development.

Stuart and Ding (2006) show that a faculty member's transition to entrepreneurial science is more straightforward in universities where the phenomenon of academic entrepreneurship is well known because it is easier to follow a path than to break one: when a colleague in the same department has transitioned to commercial science, he is able to provide advice on practical matters, including how to have relationship with the university's technology transfer office and he could assume the role of mentor or investor to support a firm started by a colleague (Shane & Stuart, 2002). In addition, scientists with co-authors who had become academic entrepreneurs were more likely to become entrepreneurs themselves.

In this sense, working in an entrepreneurial university fosters the emergence of new academic entrepreneurs, but, as hypothesized by Cooper and Bruno (1977, p. 21), "for a new, high technology firm, the primary assets are the knowledge and skills of the founders. Any competitive advantage the new firm achieves is likely to be based upon what the founders can do better than others". The stock of human capital and social capital of researchers positively influences the transition to entrepreneurship (Ding, 2011; Varga, 2006).

To succeed in the creation and development of a new firm, an individual must have had the capacity to mobilize resources. Star scientists have the reputations to attract the interest of potential investors.

To measure human capital, scholars suggest to use the number of publication, which is a common way of knowledge transfer (Landry, Amara, & Rherrad, 2006) and a way for gaining legitimacy in academia (Judge, Cable, Colbert, & Rynes, 2007). Legitimacy plays an important role in new venture creation due to the fact that it reduces the pressure of the so-called liabilities of newness (Scholten, Omta, Kemp, & Elfring, 2015). This concept concerns the fact that a new firm suffers from an initial lack of legitimacy (Karlsson & Wigren, 2012) and a lack of experience in production, product development and organizational structure. These make it more difficult for entrepreneurs to access resources.

Concerning the human capital of researchers, business education and business experience are considered important factors for the creation and management of a new business. There is empirical evidence of the lack of necessary commercial skills to run a business among researchers. In this sense, specific courses can increase the performance of spin-off companies.

In the identification of opportunities within the market, it is important to have business experience and not only a business education. In fact, academic founders with prior industrial experience have more capacity to understand the potential commercial viability of their research (Shane, 2004).

D'Este et al. (2010) show that the prior knowledge of markets and customers has a positive impact on the valorization within the market of new discoveries by academic researchers (Shane, 2000).

These findings indicate that academics who have acquired multiple knowledge in their research activities are able to find associations between their researches and business activities related to them and they will be better prepared to exploit the commercial opportunities resulting from their research than other colleagues more specialized in a unique field (Bercovitz & Feldmann, 2006).

Another important personal asset of the academic entrepreneur is the years of experience (Louis, Blumenthal, Gluck, & Stoto, 1989; Ucbasaran, Westhead, & Wright, 2007) that could be an indication of opportunities of prior learning in knowledge transfer and commercialization of research.

Even the participation in research collaborations improves the possibility that an academic becomes an entrepreneur due to the fact that she/he could be more capable of accessing complementary expertise in order to acquire additional equipment and most of all additional resources (Bammer, 2008).

Another factor linked to academic entrepreneurs is social capital that is often mentioned as an important factor that influences the development of companies (Czarnitzki, Rammer, & Toole, 2014; Landry et al., 2006).

Social capital is defined as the contacts an individual has with his/her environment.

University employees are often involved in research projects funded by external actors such as firms, governmental bodies, etc. These types of cooperation are often based on a previous relationship.

4 Academic Spin-Offs in Italy

In the following, I identify the variables determining growth processes of academic spin-offs in the Italian context, with a specific focus on academic spin-offs of Università Politecnica delle Marche.

The growth patterns of academic ASOs is related to the characteristics of the entrepreneurs, of the firms and of the university (Delmar, Davidsson, & Gartner, 2003); including the external context, such as VC availability, supporting services, economic situation, market and technology opportunities or relationships with industry (Chiesa & Piccaluga, 2000).

What I wish to do is to understand growth phenomena, taking into consideration several factors such as sectors of activities, geographical concentration and ownership structure.

The paragraph is organized as follows: the first section presents an overview of theoretical approaches which can help in the identification of critical factors for the growth of academic spin-offs, the second section of the chapter is focused on the experience of Italian spin-offs, with specific regard to the process of growth, while the third section shows the impact of academic spin-offs on local economies.

4.1 *Theoretical Approaches*

In the literature, many scholars have developed different theoretical approaches which can help in the identification of critical factors for the growth of academic spin-offs: the Resource-Based View, the Market-Led Perspective and the Institutional Link Perspective.

The Resource-Based View (RBV) was introduced by Penrose (1959). According to the RBV, firms are bundles of assets or resources possessed by the firm management. The RBV suggests that resources have to be unique to firms in order to create competitive advantage and their heterogeneity is a necessary but not sufficient condition.

Firm resources are classified into four categories: financial, physical, human and organizational. For a high-tech start-up, financial resources are especially important to acquire and develop physical assets (e.g. machinery, equipment, distribution channels) and intangible ones (e.g. brand, patents).

Firm-specific resources can be knowledge-based or property-based. Property-based resources refer to tangible inputs, whereas knowledge-based resources describe the ways in which firms combine and use their tangible inputs (Galunic & Rodan, 1998). Knowledge-based resources are difficult to imitate and thus could generate sustainable competitive advantage (Wiklund & Shepherd, 2003).

According to the RBV, spin-off performance depends on the characteristics of the firm's resources (human resources, technology and financial resources).

By adopting a Market-Led Perspective, the competitive strategy should be niche strategy versus diversification strategy and local approach versus international and global approach (Porter, 1980).

The Institutional Link Perspective considers the influence of institutional context (in terms of culture, rules and incentive system) on the spin-offs' growth processes (Dacin, 1997).

I adopt in the following the first theoretical approach.

4.2 *Characteristics of Academic Spin-Offs in Italy*

In Italy the phenomenon of university spin-offs started to be relevant in the early years of 2000s, partly as a result of regulatory changes that introduced the possibility for universities and research institutions to authorize their staff to participate in business ventures for the exploitation of research results.

The role of universities in the creation and diffusion of knowledge and in fostering a region's capacity of innovation becomes clear in the mid-Nineties due to the fact that a significant proportion of academic innovation remained not valorized within the market, the so-called European Paradox (Rodríguez-Navarro & Narin, 2018). In this sense, most universities have progressively realized the exploitation potential of their research results and started to promote and sustain the creation of new ventures (Cesaroni & Piccaluga, 2005). Moreover, policymakers started to change the national legislative with specific laws to facilitate TT activities from universities, and in particular, to support the creation of academic spin-offs.

Only since the early 2000s, following the adoption of a specific legislation, has the phenomenon of research spin-off become significant. In particular, art. 2 of the DLG. July 27, 1999 n. 297 authorizes universities and other public research institutions (PRI) to issue regulations that allow researchers and professors, as an exception to existing rules, to participate in the capital and the management of newly established companies aimed at the industrial use of research. With the Ministerial Decree N. 593 of 8/8/2000 procedures were defined for the granting of concessions under Legislative Decree 297/1999. Following this legislation, in the early years of the decade, the PRI developed specific regulations governing the involvement of their permanent (such as professors and researchers) and temporary staff (such as doctoral students, research grant holders, etc.) in spin-off companies (Muscio, Quaglione, & Ramaciotti, 2016). These regulations also allow universities to supply services to support spin-offs before and after they are established (start-up or incubation). For this reason, in the first years of activity (usually the first three), spin-off companies have the opportunity to grow in a "protected environment" thanks to both the free services that many universities provide, and to the possibility of using staff and research facilities free of charge or at lower than market prices. In most cases this "incubation" of new initiatives is undertaken directly, taking advantage of the research facilities at the institution where the lecturers and researchers involved in the initiative are employed; in other cases ad hoc structures have been created with the support of public agencies in the area. The PRI may also participate with minority shares in the capital of the new company. The latter aspect is influenced by the importance that the individual agency intends to assign to this instrument of technology transfer and by the consequent support policies implemented (Iacobucci et al., 2011).

For information about ASOs in Italian universities, I use a database jointly developed by the Center for Innovation and Entrepreneurship of the Università Politecnica delle Marche and Scuola Superiore Sant'Anna in collaboration with Netval (the database is publicly accessible at: www.spinoffitalia.it). The database contains data about the characteristics of Italian ASOs—i.e. name, year of foundation, university of foundation, sector of activity, location, etc.—and data on their economic performance (sales, profits, employees, etc.). Figure 1 shows the number of Spin-offs set up in Italy, Fig. 2 shows the distribution by sectors of activities and Fig. 3 the number of spin-offs by universities of foundation.

Academic spin-offs in Italy are characterized by a high (about 97%) survival rate and they tend to remain small (they rarely employ more than ten people) (Cesaroni & Piccaluga, 2005).

Nevertheless, the academic spin-off is a phenomenon with significant potential for Italy, most of all in view of the need for Italian businesses to change from so-called "traditional" or "low-tech" sectors to "high-tech" sectors, according to the OECD classification (OECD, 2005), or "science-based" sectors according to Pavitt's classification (Pavitt, 1984).

The effective capacity of the spin-off phenomenon to contribute to these objectives, and to have a significant impact on regional systems depends on two aspects: (a) the capacity for rapid growth of at least some of these initiatives, (b) the generation of positive externalities in the system, also by stimulating innovation in sectors which are already present in the area.

The aim of the following paragraph is to analyse the characteristics of Italian spin-offs, with specific reference to their capacity for growth.

The analysis is based on a sample of 210 spin-offs created between 2000 and 2006 for which balance sheet data were examined. Spin-offs established more recently were excluded from the analysis as they are too young for their growth process to be analysed. The analysis of the ownership team, and its change over time, was made through an examination of information provided by Chambers of Commerce.

The section is organized as follows: an overview of the phenomenon of research spin-offs in Italy in the period 2000–2007, including some information about the regulations, an analysis of the characteristics of a sample of the population of Italian spin-offs, with specific focus on issues relating to the ownership of spin-offs, and some conclusions about the factors affecting the set-up and growth process of these firms.

Number of spin-offs	**Number**
within 1979	1
1980-1989	5
1990-1999	37
2000	26
2001	29
2002	13
2003	36
2004	43
2005	52
2006	60
2007	83
2008	72
2009	75
2010	101
2011	101
2012	*135*
2013	*120*
2014	*130*
2015	*127*
2016	*101*
2017	*26*
Total number of spin-offs in 2017	***1.373***

Fig. 1 Number of Italian spin-offs by year of foundation (*Sources* https://www.spinoffitalia.it)

Sector of activities	Number	%
Innovation service	363	26,4
ICT	303	22,1
Energy and enviromental	229	16,7
Life sciences	210	15,3
Biomedical	87	6,3
Elettronics	68	5,0
Industrial automation	53	3,9
Nanotech	34	2,5
Cultural sector	22	1,6
Aerospace	4	0,3
Total number of spin-offs in 2017	***1.373***	***100,0***

Fig. 2 The distribution of spin-offs by sector of activities (*Sources* https://www.spinoffitalia.it)

4.2.1 Population and Sample

In the empirical analysis I study the period 2000–2008. Considering the birthrate of spin-offs in the time period indicated, it can be noted that since 2003 there has been a real spread of this phenomenon in Italian Public Research Institutes (PRI). The birthrate reached a first peak in 2004, suggesting a boom effect generated by the introduction of this model in the Italian system; this is seen especially in the PRI which are more sensitive to this form of research exploitation, in line with American and British models. In subsequent years, the slow down of the phenomenon can be justified by a more rigorous regulation of spin-off authorization adopted by the competent bodies through the introduction of stricter selection criteria (Fig. 4).

There is a strong concentration of spin-offs at regional level, with most initiatives being in the Center and Northern parts of the country. As observed in other countries, spin-offs are not uniformly distributed between the different PRI: the 5 most important PRI has developed about one-third of the initiatives; in addition, 80% of the spin-offs can be traced back to the first 18 PRI (Fig. 5).

PRI of foundation	n	PRI of foundation	n
CNR	75	IIT	15
Politecnico di Torino	74	Università dell'Aquila	14
Università di Genova	51	Università di Messina	14
Università di Padova	48	ENEA	13
Scuola Superiore Sant'Anna	48	Università di Sassari	13
Università di Firenze	43	Università di Trento	13
Università di Pisa	42	Università di Sannio	12
Università di Roma "Tor Vergata"	42	Università di Napoli "Federico II"	12
Politecnico di Milano	41	Università della Basilicata	12
Università del Salento	37	Università di Venezia "Ca' Foscari"	10
Università di Udine	37	Università della Tuscia	9
Università di Perugia	37	Università di Brescia	9
Università di Torino	36	Università del Molise	8
Università di Bologna	35	Università Cattolica del Sacro Cuore	8
Università Politecnica delle Marche	34	Università di Urbino	8
Università della Calabria	34	Università di Foggia	7
Università di Cagliari	28	Seconda Università di Napoli	7
Università di Siena	26	Università di Cassino	7
Università di Parma	26	Università di Bergamo	6
Università di Modena e Reggio Emilia	24	Università 'Insubria' di Varese-Como	6
Università di Pavia	24	Università San Raffaele di Milano	5
Università di Salerno	24	Università di Teramo	5
Università di Milano	22	CISE	4
Università di Trieste	22	Università di Roma Tre	4
Università di Palermo	21	CRO	4
Università di Ferrara	20	SISSA - Trieste	3
Università del Piemonte Orientale	20	Università di Macerata	3
Università di Bari	19	Fondazione Ca' Granda	2
Università di Roma "La Sapienza"	19	Università Campus Bio-Medico di Roma	2
Politecnico di Bari	19	INAF - Istituto Nazionale di Astro-Fisica	1
Università di Catania	19	Università 'Magna Grecia' di Catanzaro	1
Università di Verona	19	CREA	1
Università di Camerino	18	INFN	1
Università di Milano-Bicocca	17	IMT	1
Università di Chieti	16	Università IUAV di Venezia	1
Fondazione Bruno Kessler	15	***Total number of spin-offs in 2017***	***1.373***

Fig. 3 Number of spin-offs by university of foundation (*Sources* https://www.spinoffitalia.it)

The activity of the spin-offs by sector shows a stronger concentration in services than in manufacturing: 44% of the spin-offs operate in the field "Other business services", followed by "Computer and related activities" which account for 22% and "Research and Development" accounting for 12% of the total (Table 3).

The high concentration in business service activities and R&D is one of the main issues debated in relation to the phenomenon of spin-offs. In fact these activities are rather problematic for the growth prospects of the spin-offs themselves. In the first case there may be potential conflicts

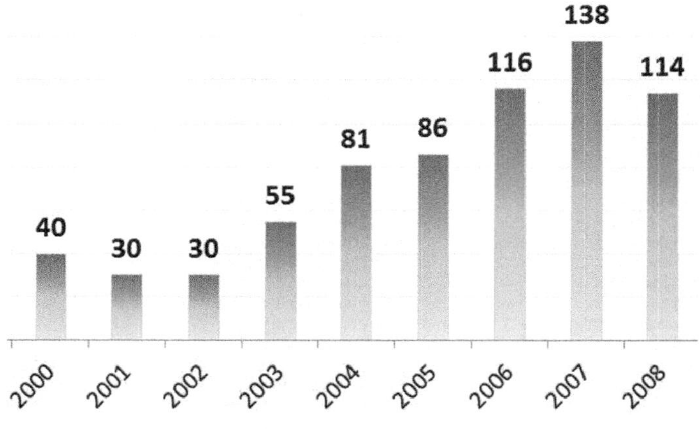

Fig. 4 Spin-offs set up in the period 2000–2008 (*Sources* https://www.spinoffitalia.it)

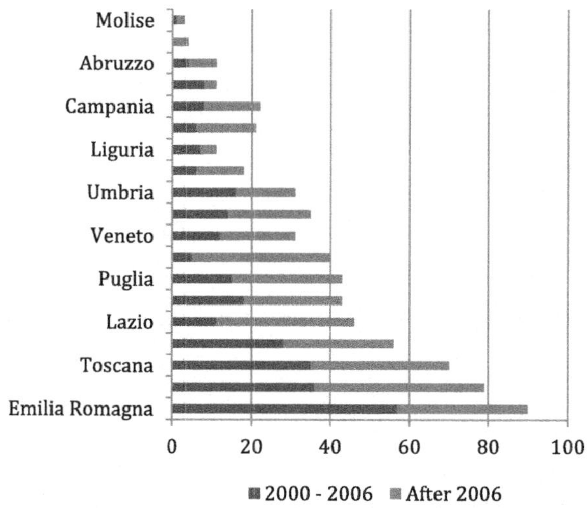

Fig. 5 Spin-offs set up in the period 2000–2008 by Region (*Sources* https://www.spinoffitalia.it)

Table 3 Sector of activity of spin-offs

Sector	*%*
R&D and services	44.1
ICT	22.2
Biomedical	9.8
Chemicals and pharmaceuticals	7.0
Electronics and telecommunications	4.8
Machinery	1.3
Transportation	3.2
Other sectors	76
Total	100

Sources https://www.spinoffitalia.it

of interest between the activities carried out by the spin-off and the institutional research activities carried out by researchers. Moreover, greater commercial orientation of university research may inhibit knowledge transfer to local high-tech start-ups. Universities interested in attracting private research sponsorship might offer sponsoring firms privileged access to the results of academic research. Universities could even assign intellectual property (IP) rights to the firms that funded the research that produced such IP. Existing firms are more motivated than universities to protect IP from public disclosure and secure exploitation rights of research results, firms want to ensure that knowledge is protected until a patent application or the research results are exploited commercially. To achieve this, firms may try to inhibit premature publication or dissemination of research results. This clearly hinders the generation of positive externalities to other firms from university research and, consequently, has negative effects on the growth potential of local high-tech start-ups. Moreover, service sector activities are fundamentally linked to the skills of the sponsors and, for that reason, the growth potential of these activities is strongly conditioned by the availability of man-days which the sponsors can sell. For this reason, some organizations have placed more stringent constraints on the activities conducted by their spin-offs and on the conditions to authorize their set up. For example, the Politecnico di Milano authorizes initiatives within the manufacturing sector and in the presence of patents. Nevertheless, in recent years the proportion of spin-offs in the service sector has grown. The increasing importance of the service sector in advanced economies is undoubtedly one of the reasons that explains the preference for services rather than for manufacturing; service activities also require less start-up capital and have a more immediate marketability of the skills acquired in academic research (Acs, Desai, & Hessels, 2008).

Both in the case of manufacturing activities and in the case of business services, technological fields of activity with a high level of know-how are clearly predominant: information technology, multimedia, energy and the environment, electronics, biotechnology and biomedical science (Acs et al., 2008).

From the methodological point of view, the analysis of growth processes was performed using the financial information for the spin-offs in their third, fifth and seventh year of business. The reason for the choice of this time span is attributable to the desire to study the growth capacity of these companies once they go beyond their incubation period within the PRI (about 3 years). In the period in which I conducted the analysis the latest balance sheet data available refer to 2009, so the information was available only for spin-offs founded in 2000 and 2006.

This methodological choice implies the loss of part of the population, namely the spin-offs created after 2006. Therefore, the sample was made up of 250 spin-offs: for 40 spin-offs (those created in 2006) data were available for the third year after set-up, for 95 spin-offs (those created between 2004 and 2005) data were available for the third and fifth year after set-up and for 75 (those set up in 2000 and 2001) data were available for the third, fifth and seventh year after the set-up (Table 4). 12 spin-offs were excluded from the sample due to cessation and 28 due to lack of information.

Table 4 Spin-offs included in the sample by year of foundation

Year of foundation	*Year of balance sheet data*								
	2002	*2003*	*2004*	*2005*	*2006*	*2007*	*2008*	*2009*	*Total observations*
2000	11		11		11				33
2001		10		10		10			30
2002			14		14		14		42
2003				40		40		40	120
2004					51		51		102
2005						44		44	88
2006							40		40
Total observations	11	10	25	50	76	94	105	84	455

Source UPM Spin-off database

Table 5 Spin-off economic activity in the sample for geographical area

Sectors	*Number of spin-offs*	*%*	*% North West*	*% North East*	*% Centre*	*% South & Islands*
Life science	68	32.9	6.3	15.5	8.2	2.9
ICT	40	19.3	5.8	3.9	4.3	5.3
R&D and services	33	15.9	1.4	8.2	5.3	1.0
Energy	21	10.1	3.4	1.9	4.3	0.5
Electronics	13	6.3	1.9	2.9	1.0	0.5
Biomedical	11	5.3	1	1.9	2.4	
Machinery	5	2.4	0.5	0.5	1.4	
Nanotechnologies	3	1.4	0	0.5	1.0	
Printing and publishing	3	1.4	0.5	1.0		
Aerospace	1	0.5	0.5			
Others	9	4.3	1.4	1.0	1.4	0.5
Total	207	100	22.7	37.2	29.5	10.6

Source UPM Spin-off database

The composition of the sample population at sectoral level and for geographical areas is shown in (Table 5).

The sectors of life science and ICT are prevalent in the North West area and in the South and Islands. In the Centre there is a concentration of companies focused on R&D and services, while in the North East there is a high concentration in the life science sector.

4.2.2 *Size and Growth Process*

The first aspect analysed is related to the volume of sales recorded by the sample companies after three years of activity, i.e. after the incubation period. Given the nature of these enterprises, their success on the market is critically important for assessing their capacity to exploit research results. The distribution of firms is skewed with respect to the average with most of the spin-offs being concentrated in lower-level sales classes while only a few have a high turnover level.

Three years after their creation almost 50% of the spin-offs have consolidated a turnover volume of less than 100,000 euros. Of these, nearly two-thirds have turnover values below 50,000 euros. This seems to highlight the initial difficulties encountered by a significant proportion of spin-offs in implementing innovative ideas in order to develop a business which is really valid and competitive on the market (Table 6).

Table 6 Spin-offs by class of sales in the third, fifth and seventh year of activity (thousands of Euro)

Class of sales	*III year*		*V year*		*VII year*	
	Number of spin-offs	%	*Number of spin-offs*	%	*Number of spin-offs*	%
>1000	7	3	6	4	5	7
500–999	10	5	19	11	8	11
250–499	23	11	27	16	16	21
100–250	59	28	48	28	18	24
50–99	38	18	23	14	8	11
0–49	73	35	47	28	20	27
Total	210	100	170	100	75	100

Source UPM Spin-off database

The data, although apparently negative, should be interpreted in the context of the normal difficulties that new businesses face during start-up and that lead to high mortality rates in all sectors of activity. Moreover, these difficulties are greater for new companies in high technology sectors, as is the case for the research spin-offs with a corporate structure involving people with different skills and expectations.

28% of the companies are situated in the middle segment, with sales ranging from 100 to 250 thousand euros, while in the third year a good percentage of firms (11%) already have a level of turnover in the range 250–500 thousand euros.

The distribution of the spin-off by turnover 5 years after set-up shows, as might be expected, a general transition to higher levels of sales. However, it is interesting to note that the growth capacity appears to be greater for firms of more recent origin. The percentage composition of the sample analysed in the fifth year by level of turnover seems to reflect the data sample for the third year, also considering the possible effect of selection during this two year period for those firms which were less successful on the market.

The analysis of turnover for the fifth year of activity can provide additional food for thought in view of the fact that the period between years 3 and 5 is considered the time frame of reference for institutional investors operating in the field of innovative start-ups.

Of the 170 companies observed, 3% had a growth path that could potentially attract the interest of these investors. However, it should be noted that even this figure appears to be lower than the target goal of the venture capitalists. After seven years after start-up, the number of spin-offs that could potentially attract the interest of investors increases from 3 to 7%.

Apart from the growth of sales, another important aspect of spin-off growth is the ability to create jobs. Since the data concerning staff are not always given in the balance sheet notes, the amount of personnel costs was used as a proxy for wage and salary employment. The data shows how in the third year of activity the spin-offs have, to a certain extent, postponed some choices related to the organization of the company (in terms of human resources), sometimes even in the presence of a revenue which would be sufficient to justify them: 44% of spin-offs has no personnel costs (Table 7). The choices made by companies do not appear to be consistent with the conditions that should characterize the third year of these companies; from the fourth year onwards, in fact, the spin-off companies usually end the university incubation period and therefore might be expected to make clear organizational choices. Five years after the set-up, the data doesn't change significantly. The distribution of the spin-off by personnel costs 7 years after set-up shows, as might be expected, a general transition to higher levels of sales, even if 30% of them still does not have salaried employees. These spin-offs have not implemented meaningful growth processes and maintain a generally cautious approach in structuring the organization.

Table 7 Number of spin-offs and percentage by personnel costs value in the three, five and seven year of activity (thousands of Euro)

Class of personnel costs	*III year*		*V year*		*VII year*	
	Number of spin-offs	*%*	*Number of spin-offs*	*%*	*Number of spin-offs*	*%*
>500			4	2	8	11
250–499	6	3	11	6	6	8
100–250	15	7	23	14	8	11
50–99	19	9	17	10	7	9
0–49	78	37	52	31	24	32
0	92	44	63	37	22	29
Total	210	100	170	100	75	100

Source UPM Spin-off database

4.2.3 Governance

Almost all the research spin-offs have the legal status of limited liability companies, with a few exceptions of corporations and cooperative companies. The use of the legal status of a limited liability company is associated with a relatively limited initial endowment of capital, generally close to the minimum required for limited companies. Three years after set-up, the average stock capital continues to be relatively low (approximately 40 thousand euros), although there is still a good growth rate so that in 6% of cases, after three years the stock capital exceeds 100,000 euros (Table 8).

Five years after set-up, the average stock capital increases (approximately 55 thousand euros); as a result of that spin-offs in the class 11–49 increase from 37 to 45% and 8% of cases exceeds 100,000 euros (Table 9).

Seven years after set-up, the average stock capital increases (approximately 100 thousand euros), due to the fact that the class 50–99, 100–499 and 500–999 reach 33% of sample (Table 10).

The ownership structure of the spin-off is, in most cases, made up mainly by individual partners. These are supported by PRI shares, companies, finance companies and other institutions. With reference to the ownership structure (Table 11) summarizes the stock ownership of institutional shareholders (not individuals) at set-up.

The data show a clear difference between the financial commitment of the PRI and the other two types of investors. PRI are present in

Table 8 Stock capital of the spin-off in the third year of activity (thousands of Euro)

Year of foundation	*Stock capital*					*Number of spin-offs per year of foundation*
	10 (%)	*11–49 (%)*	*50–99 (%)*	*100–499 (%)*	*500–999 (%)*	
2000		64	27	9	0	11
2001	30	40	20	10	0	10
2002	36	50	7	7	0	14
2003	35	38	15	13	0	40
2004	35	37	24	4	0	51
2005	43	39	16	2	0	44
2006	63	28	5	5	0	40
Total	40	38	16	6	0	210

Source UPM Spin-off database

Table 9 Share capital of the spin-off in the fifth year of activity (thousands of Euro)

Year of foundation	*Capital*					*Number of spin-offs per year of foundation*
	10 (%)	*11–49 (%)*	*50–99 (%)*	*100–499 (%)*	*500–999 (%)*	
2000	0	55	18	27	0	11
2001	10	60	20	0	10	10
2002	36	50	7	7	0	14
2003	30	43	10	15	3	40
2004	31	39	24	6	0	51
2005	34	45	18	2	0	44
Total	29	45	17	8	1	170

Source UPM Spin-off database

Table 10 Share capital of the spin-off in the seventh year of activity (thousands of euros)

Year of Foundation	*Capital*					*Number of spin-offs per year of foundation*
	10 (%)	*11–49 (%)*	*50–99 (%)*	*100–499 (%)*	*500–999 (%)*	
2000		45	18	36		11
2001		60	30		10	10
2002	36	50	7		7	14
2003	28	40	10	18	5	40
Total	21	45	13	15	5	75

Source UPM Spin-off database

Table 11 Spin-offs by ownership share of universities, companies and financial institutions at set-up (percentage of total)

Share of legal entity owners	*0*	*<10*	*10–19*	*20–49*	*>50*	*Total*
PRI	50	15	32	2	1	100
Companies	60	4	7	17	12	100
Financial companies or other institutions	91	2	3	2	2	100

Source UPM Spin-off database

52% of the spin-offs with an average share of about 10% and a participation value of around 5000 euros. This is because the PRI generally enter into the capital of the spin-offs at the time of their creation and with a clearly minority share; the main purpose behind this presence is, in fact, to provide credibility for the new initiative rather than to enhance the investment. Ferretti, Ferri, Fiorentino, Parmentola, and Sapio (2019) suggest that the engagement of the parent university in the ownership structure of ASOs has a not statistically significant effect. Some studies show that ASOs in which the university is involved in ownership structure have a worse performance than ASOs in which university is not present (Bonardo, Paleari, & Vismara, 2011). A possible explanation could be that the presence of an university that has a large share of capital can reduce the possibility of spin-offs in terms of their attractiveness to venture capitalists (Fini, Fu, Mathisen, Rasmussen, & Wright, 2017).

In the case of firms and financial companies, entry in order to exploit the capital is prevalent. This leads to greater selectivity in entry and a greater financial commitment. If we analyse the spin-offs where there is the presence of industrial companies in social capital, in 41% of cases the share of capital is in class 20–49, while in 31% of cases it is more then 50%.

The information provided by the Chambers of Commerce allows not only the reconstruction of the governance structure at set-up but also of the subsequent amendments. The stock capital increases for 35 spin-offs and this leads to an increase in revenues and profits. The analysis of the financial information of the spin-off companies in which the share of capital held by companies or institutions is significant (above 20%) shows that in 65% of cases, this generated an increase in sales revenues and an increase in personnel expenses. This phenomenon is explained by the fact that the entry of outside investors occurred during the start-up with the aim of financing investments needed for the subsequent development of the spin-off.

Finance is a catalyst of this wealth creation yet access to venture capital is a major impediment faced by spin-offs (Wright, Lockett, Clarysse, & Binks, 2006). In line with the pecking order theory, venture capitalists prefer to invest after the seed stage, the financial resources are more important in the previous phases.

The aim of this study is to evaluate the factors affecting the process of growth of academic spin-offs in Italy. From a quantitative point of view, measurable through variables such as turnover or employment, the impact is rather marginal. Analysis of the growth process of Italian spin-offs set up between 2000 and 2006 finds that only a low percentage of them showed a significant growth; most of the spin-offs have difficulty in transforming the initial idea into a sustainable business.

The empirical analysis confirms the results of De Turi and Garzoni (2018) who, analysing a sample of Italian ASOs between 2001 and 2017, find that the impact of spin-offs on the local economy is rather small at quantitative level.

The pattern of growth that can be expected for these companies is characterized by a high risk of failure and by a few instances of significant success.

Two aspects of the Italian situation are different from that of other countries, especially the UK and the US: the first is the low rate of failure at three and five years after set-up (in our sample we observed the closing of spin-offs only in 5% of cases); the second is the lack of high-growth companies, even many years after start-up. These two aspects are linked because they are both a result of the unwillingness of the spin-off to take risks through significant capital investment. This finding could be linked to the characteristics of the spin-offs and to the context in which they operate. Many of the spin-off companies are engaged in business services and these activities are characterized by low initial investment and low growth prospects. As regards the Italian institutional context, the main problem is the difficulty for new firms to raise adequate funds during their start-up and subsequent development. Given the nature of these initiatives, the appropriate form of financing is that of equity capital provided by specialized investors (venture capital). The size of this market in Italy is still modest. One possible solution to this problem may be to set up a closer collaboration between spin-offs and established businesses, which may find technological or commercial synergies with the new ventures. In this regard there are some interesting examples of spin-off's customers or partner companies that have acquired shares of capital in order to sustain the development of the spin-off. The possibility to grow depends on the environment of spin-offs and on the interaction with external partners including friends, family, colleagues and academicians who provide access to important resources (Birley, 1985).

In this respect, networks are an essential factor influencing the survival of academic spin-offs (Soetanto, 2009) and they should receive considerable attention by incubator organizations in designing support policies (Hoang & Antoncic, 2003). Networks provide entrepreneurs with a variety of resources, such as market information, problem-solving support, social support, venture funding (Nicolaou & Birley, 2003).

The problems in raising equity capital arise not only from the supply side but also from the demand side. Many spin-offs, especially in services, do not have enough growth prospects to make them attractive for an outside investor. Moreover, in these cases, the market prospects of the spin-offs are too dependent on the competences of the promoters and lack a well-defined product or service which can be standardized and replicable.

A previous study conducted on the characteristics of an entrepreneurial team that promoted the spin-offs shows the importance of entrepreneurial organizational factors during the phases of start-up and development of academic spin-offs (Iacobucci et al., 2011). In organizational and business terms, the analysis identified two main problems: the imbalance of the sponsor team towards technical skills and lack of clarity in the identification of the entrepreneurial figure. As regards the first aspect, there is a lack of personnel with skills which are complementary to technical ones, particularly managerial and commercial skills. The lack of personnel with management skills could be balanced by recruiting staff with appropriate characteristics. However, this is hampered by the difficulty that the spin-off has in investing in the organizational structure during the early stages of start-up. On the contrary, what cannot be balanced is the motivation for entrepreneurship, since it is closely connected with the motivation of the single promoters.

The reason could be the fact that an academic entrepreneur seeks to protect and negotiate his positions, making sense of his professional role identities.

The limited propensity for entrepreneurship of the promoters is a recurring problem in the spin-off companies investigated. In this sense, the governance of spin-offs could represent an obstacle to growth and development. Personal abilities, commitments and individual attitudes are seen to be critical factors in successful academic spin-offs. The core aspect of the firms surveyed in this section is the transformation of scientific knowledge developed in the universities into useful knowledge to create competitive products for the market. The key problem in the start-up of academic spin-offs is the difficulty to transform academic knowledge into management and organizational objectives. This finding is confirmed by the literature: the majority of academic spin-offs are started by purely technical founding teams, often lacking in market orientation. The importance of having an industrial partner taking an equity stake in the spin-offs is still often undervalued by technical entrepreneurs, TTOs and policymakers (Ben-Hafaïedh et al., 2018). Prospective entrepreneurs should first assess their own readiness for starting a new business, by checking their market competencies and—if lacking—by (eventually) waiting for an industrial partner or building a proper set of their own skills before creating the new venture.

This does not imply that the firm's performances should be attributed only to the entrepreneurial characteristics; the technical knowledge of the founder-entrepreneur plays a crucial role during the first stage of the firm's life, but during the growth stage, a more complex set of resources is necessary to sustain the firm's activities, and the main issues regard availability of financial resources, organizational weaknesses, availability of specialized suppliers, availability of professional services. The lack of these factors generates a vicious circle where the low level of investment and commitment creates low revenue and consequent scant capacity to stimulate employment, affecting the business size and the economic role played by academic spin-offs.

According to the literature, an empirical evidence for spin-offs set up in 2000–2008 is that the formal involvement of an industrial partner and of a financial partner among the company's shareholders have a significant impact on growth. The localization of spin-offs in a metropolitan area and the concentration of hi-tech firms in a specific context, such as the North areas have a positive impact on growth as well.

4.3 *The Local Impact of Academic Spin-Offs*

The last part of this book analyses the impact at regional level of academic spin-offs and discusses how to measure it using empirical data of a specific context: Marche Region and its most important University, Università Politecnica delle Marche. The Italian experience shown in the prior section, confirms that the quantitative impact of spin-offs on local economies is rather low; however, there are qualitative direct and indirect effects that must be taken into consideration in the short and in the longer term.

According to regional studies, the impact of spin-offs tends to be local as most spin-offs stay within the same geographical area as the institution from which they originated (Shane, 2004). To the best of my knowledge, little attention has been paid to evaluate the role of spin-offs on technology transfer activity by universities and to their impact on local systems (De Turi & Garzoni, 2018; Iacobucci & Micozzi, 2015).

The aims of the next section are to cover this knowledge gap:

a. developing an analytical framework to evaluate the impact of academic spin-offs on university technology transfer and on regional development;
b. applying this framework to the Italian context.

The empirical analysis is based on a sample of 26 spin-offs created between 2000 and 2010 from Università Politecnica delle Marche, for which balance sheet data and information about governance were examined. The analysis of the ownership and management team, and its change over time, was made through an examination of information provided by the Chambers of Commerce.

4.3.1 *Academic Entrepreneurship and Regional Growth*

The territory in the form of Regional Innovation System (Cooke, Heidenreich, & Braczyk, 2004) offers a platform for cooperation enabling the open innovation approach. In this system, several actors working towards a creation of innovations, and the University-Industry link play a fundamental role.

The growing importance of the university third mission (technology transfer) emphasizes the role played by universities at local level (Lawton Smith & Ho, 2006). In this sense, there is a need to look at the multifaceted benefits which universities bring to their territories (Boucher, Conway, & van der Meer, 2003).

This is true particularly in the case of university-firm relations, giving the importance of face-to-face interactions (Hewitt-Dundas, 2013). This is even more true in the case of spin-offs, that are normally located very close to the parent institution due to the fact that: (a) the incubator role played by universities in the start-up phase (use of university structures); (b) the involvement of academicians; (c) the continuous collaboration between spin-offs and university departments.

Empirical literature finding supports this line of research giving growing importance to consider the knowledge spillovers from university research to localized industrial innovation (Audretsch & Feldman, 1996). All potential benefits found in the literature are analysed in the following section to evaluate the quantitative and qualitative impact on a specific local context, using the case study of Università Politecnica delle Marche.

4.3.2 The Case Study of Università Politecnica Delle Marche

In Marche region there are 4 universities (Table 12), the most important one is Università Politecnica delle Marche. The data refers to 2010.

In the first decade after the legislation (2001–2010), 26 spin-offs were set-up by professors and researchers of Università Politecnica delle Marche, 4 of these are dissolved or in liquidation (Fig. 6).

Table 12 Universities in Marche Region

	Università Politecnica delle Marche	*Università degli Studi di Urbino*	*Università degli studi di Macerata*	*Università di Camerino*
Students	16,400	12,500	10,500	6400
Researchers	523	420	316	280
Spin-offs	26	6	2	0

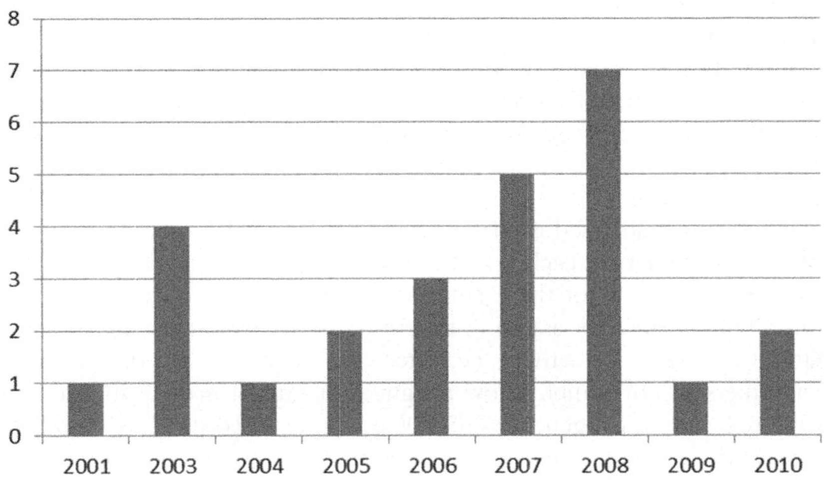

Fig. 6 Univpm spin-offs by founding year (*Source* UPM Spin-off database)

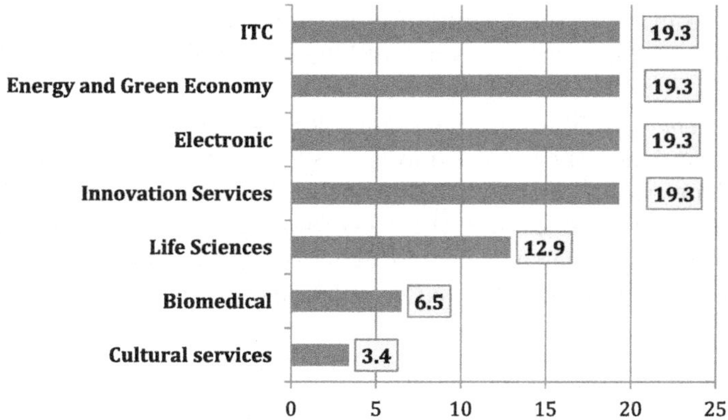

Fig. 7 Univpm spin-off companies by sector (*Source* UPM Spin-off database)

The prevalent sectors of activities are, as expected, ICT, energy and green economies and innovation services and this reflect the sectors of activities of Università Politecnica delle Marche (Fig. 7).

The concentration in high-tech sectors is particularly important for the region in the view of the need for Marche businesses to change their specialization from low tech to knowledge-based sector.

Over the last decades we observe in the Marche region a decrease of employment in manufacturing in low-tech sectors and a progressive shift from this one to other sectors, but the process is slow.

4.3.3 Revenues

The first aspect analysed is related to the volume of sales recorded by the sample companies for each year after the set-up.

Given the nature of these enterprises, their success on the market is critically important for assessing their capacity to exploit research results. After three years of activity, i.e. after the incubation period, the best performers of our sample show a significant rate of growth in sales. In 2001 only, a spin-off generates 65,000 euros. In 2010 the 23 spin-offs of Università Politecnica delle Marche have a total revenue of more than 5 million euros (Table 13).

The best performers of the sample show a continuous process of growth with the exception of EcoTechSystem and BINT that operate in the service sectors (Fig. 8).

Table 13 Revenues of spin-offs of Università Politecnica delle Marche

Spin-off	*Year of foundation*	*2001*	*2002*	*2003*	*2004*	*2005*	*2006*	*2007*	*2008*	*2009*	*2010*
Nautes S.r.l.	2001	65.4	260.7	389	513.4	578.3	731.5	971.3	1146.8	1116.6	1234.1
Strategie S.r.l.	2005					32.4	171.4	457.4	434.1	563.3	567.8
P.C.Q. S.r.l.	2007							26.5	219	386.4	438.4
Duepuntozero S.r.l.	2008								70	378.3	437.5
A.M.A. S.r.l.	2008								33	46.3	326.5
L.I.V.E. S.r.l.	2007							121.2	313.6	280.6	324.1
ArieLAB S.r.l.	2004					12	28.5	39.2	172.6	152.5	274.8
SIBE S.r.l.	2007							46.2	90.9	201.5	260.3
BINT S.r.l.	2006						294.1	426.1	229.8	291	236.6
SI2G S.r.l.	2008								23.5	49.3	209.8
EcoTechSystems S.r.l.	2003			61.7	84.8	115.1	124.4	363.7	914.2	553.6	208.3
IDEA Soc Coop.	2007							18.4	7.2	17.7	165.1
Smart Space Solutions S.r.l.	2008								10	93.1	127.7
Artemis S.r.l.	2003			68.5	19	27.7	27.1	81.1	39.9	85	120.6
NOW S.r.l.	2009									31.5	50
Tecnosuoli S.r.l.	2008								9.5	22.8	21.7
H.E.O.S. S.r.l.	2008								*	4.2	17.8
Oce. AN. Soc. Coop.	2003			1.8	23.1	30.2	133	56.8	32.5	14.8	16.6
CEDAR Solutions S.r.l.	2007							0	5.2	120.7	14.2
ASSET S.r.l.	2010										0
OPENMOB S.r.l.	2010										0
Seismotechnologies S.r.l.	2005					8	6	32	51.6	100.8	***
Ingegna S.r.l.	2006							57.6	F	–	–

(continued)

Table 13 (continued)

Spin-off	*Year of foundation*	*2001*	*2002*	*2003*	*2004*	*2005*	*2006*	*2007*	*2008*	*2009*	*2010*
VI.RA.BO. S.r.l.	2003			2	0.8	**					
Alpiquadro S.r.l.	2008								0	F	–
Thermal TI De S.r.l.	2006						0	0	F	–	–
Total revenues		65.4	260.7	523.0	641.1	803.7	1.516	2697.5	3803.4	4.510	5051.9

F failure, *S* sold out
Source UPM Spin-off database

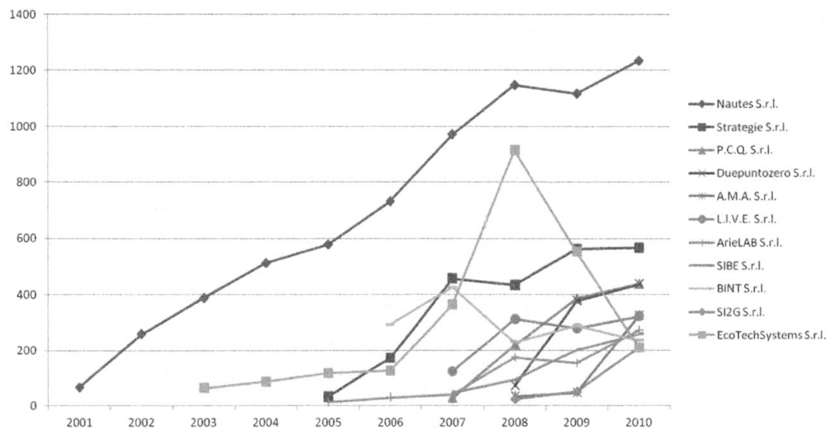

Fig. 8 Best performers of spin-offs of Università Politecnica delle Marche (*Source* UPM Spin-off database)

Apart from the growth of sales, another important aspect of spin-off growth is the ability to create jobs. Since data concerning staff are not always given in the balance sheet notes, the amount of personnel costs was used as a proxy for wage and salary employment. The data shows how the spin-offs postponed some choices related to the organization of the company (in terms of human resources), sometimes even in the presence of a revenue which would be sufficient to justify them: around 30% of our sample has no personnel costs. I try to make an estimation of how many people are employed in spin-offs. I sum the total expenditure for personnel costs and divide by 30 thousand euros, which is more or less the average salary for a full-time employee.

The obtained value is underestimated because some people in spin-offs have a collaboration contract and the item "personnel costs" in the balance sheet doesn't include it.

These spin-offs have not implemented meaningful growth processes and maintain a generally cautious approach in structuring the organization.

Considering the ownership structure, almost all the research spin-offs have the legal status of limited liability companies, with a few exceptions of corporations and cooperative companies. The use of the legal status of a limited liability company is associated with a relatively limited

Table 14 Spin-offs by ownership share of universities, companies and financial institutions at set-up (percentage of total)

Share of legal entity owners	*0*	*<10*	*10–19*	*20–49*	*>50*	*Total*
PRI	36	50	14	0	0	100
Companies	56	4	4	36	12	100
Financial companies or other institutions	100	0	0	0	0	100

Source UPM Spin-off database

initial endowment of capital, generally close to the minimum required for limited companies. Three years after set-up, the average stock capital continues to be relatively low.

The ownership structure of the spin-off is, in most cases, made up mainly by individual partners. These are supported by PRI shares, companies, finance companies and other institutions (Table 14).

The data show a clear difference between the financial commitment of the PRI and the other two types of investors. PRI are present in 64% of the spin-offs with an average share of about 10% and a participation value of around 5000 euros. This is because the PRI generally enter into the capital of the spin-offs at the time of their creation and with a clearly minority share; the main purpose behind this presence is, in fact, to provide credibility for the new initiative. In contrast, in the case of firms and financial companies, entry in order to exploit the capital is the prevalent motivation. This leads to greater selectivity in entry and a greater financial commitment. If we analyse the spin-offs where there is the presence of industrial companies in social capital, in 36% of cases the share of capital is in class 20–49, while in 12% of cases it is more then 50%.

Analysing the team of promoters, this is made up of several partners, 6 on average. Of these, 1 or 2 are faculty members that have the role of promoting the creation of spin-offs and providing professional advice based on experience, during the incubation stage, while the others are researchers or former students. This means that, at least, for each spin-off 6 people try the entrepreneurial career and the probability that an entrepreneur starts another company is higher than one who doesn't try. The findings suggest that teams evolve over time and change in composition, in this sense, many people try the entrepreneurial career.

On the basis of this data I try to identify a set of indicators to measure the impact of these 23 spin-offs on the local context.

A qualitative analysis conducted through interviews to promoters of spin-offs shows that most of the ones that have changed the team of founders have a more relevant process of growth. According to Vanaelst et al. (2006), the entrepreneurial teams evolve through the different stages of a spin-out process, suggesting that teams evolve over time and change in composition, and therefore, they cannot be studied as immutable entities.

Even in my case study teams active in the first phase of the spin-out process appear to be unbalanced in terms of experience. Their experience is highly concentrated in research and development. In this sense, teams in the first phase of the spin-out process, which are still deciding how to commercialize their knowledge, show a lack of entrepreneurial experience.

4.3.4 A System of Indicators to Evaluate the Local Impact of Academic Spin-Offs

In the literature, it is possible to identify a wide range of economic benefits that spin-offs bring to their territories:

1. they generate high-tech entrepreneurship (Etzkowitz & Leydesdorff, 2000),
2. they build new networks to access finance and to develop sales and marketing (Dahlstrand, 1999),
3. they retain close linkages with their "parent" institution, through incubators, technology transfer, recruitment of young researchers and research collaborations (Heydebreck, Klofsten, & Maier, 2000),
4. they are sources of technological spillover, and can foster the emergence of regional technology clusters (Di Gregorio & Shane, 2003),
5. they stimulate business support services and infrastructure (Lockett et al., 2003).

Starting from the potential benefits of spin-offs, I propose a set of indicators to evaluate the impact of academic spin-offs on local economies (Iacobucci & Micozzi, 2015) (Table 15).

Table 15 Set of indicators to measure the impact of academic spin-offs

Impact	*Indicators*
High-tech employer	Sector of activity Number of employees
Source of technological entrepreneurship	Sector of activity Promoters, owners, managers
Links with parent institutions	Grants and contracts with parent university
Global networks for finance, technology and markets	Ownership structure, international project in R&D, geographical market
Source of technological spillover	Collaboration at local level Labour mobility
Stimulate business support services	Incubators, start-up competitions, entrepreneurship courses

Sources Iacobucci and Micozzi (2015)

Sectors of activities, number of employees and number of promoters could measure the capability of spin-offs to create hi-tech employment and entrepreneurship.

The number of grants and of contracts with the parent university measures the links between the spin-off and PRI.

The capability of a spin-off to create global networks for finance, technology and market could be evaluated through the number of international projects in R&D, geographical market and ownership structure.

Labour mobility is an indicator of technological spillover. Inside the governance of spin-offs there is a lot of turnover in promoters, managers, researchers, etc.

The number of incubations, start-up competition and entrepreneurial education are linked with the development of spin-offs in terms of number and growth.

If we try to evaluate the impact of academic spin-offs by Università Politecnica delle Marche using the available information to measure the impact using the set of indicators we could say that it tends to be relevant but local, remaining within the same geographical area of the institution from which the spin-offs originated.

Table 16 shows the available data for 2010 of 23 spin-offs.

The analysis suggests that the phenomenon of spin-offs has positive qualitative impacts in several directions. Spin-offs can be important drivers of regional economic development because they generate hi-tech

Table 16 Impact of academic spin-offs of Università Politecnica delle Marche

Impact	*Short term*
High-tech employer (full time equivalent)	34
Source of technological entrepreneurship	136
Volume of sales	5mln
High-tech employer	ICT, energy, innovation service, life science

entrepreneurship: they are the source of 136 technology entrepreneurs that can help transforming local economies, through the emergence of local technology clusters. Furthermore, they represent a connection for other firms to access the expertise and skills within universities, encouraging the development of networks through which new technologies and knowledge can be shared. Following the "network paradigm" to analyse a territorial-system, a primary network is the one between small innovative firms and local sources of scientific knowledge such as universities and research centres. This relationship allows small firms to build up the technological environment that sustains their innovative capability. Academic spin-offs represent a significant example of network between research centres and small firms. Last but not least, they are companies in high-tech sectors, so they can contribute to production specialization to knowledge-based activities, building learning activities which improve the quality of regional innovation environment.

My results reaffirm the consolidated literature about the localized nature of knowledge transfer. If knowledge spillover tends to occur only within limited geographic areas, embedding economic activity based on this knowledge within the local context, universities can become important focal points for local economic developments.

In this sense the main results of our analysis could be summed up as follows:

1. Spin-off is not a way of commercializing university research, because the main beneficiaries (in financial terms) are former students and researchers. For the universities spin-off promotion generates costs with little prospective returns;

2. Nevertheless, this phenomenon could have positive effects at the local level but we have to evaluate it in the long term;
3. The geographical span of the spin-off impact is mainly at a local level;
4. To evaluate the real effect it is important to consider the local context in terms of industry specialization and policy objectives.

We chose to adopt a local approach due to the fact that there are several differences in local innovation systems and these may depend on the relevance of the three main actors of the triple helix model, university, industry and government, in terms of:

- quantitative importance on the regional innovation system;
- the orientation towards R&D and innovation;
- technology transfer activities by universities;
- R&D expenditures by firms;
- R&D funding;
- the relations between the three main actors;
- number and amount of university-firms relations;
- funds allocated by public institutions to firms and universities.

These differences in the local system determine the development of spin-offs due to the fact that the factors fostering the creation of this kind of firms are several. This can be important from the point of view of policymakers, concerned on fostering economic development locally, and for university administrators to decide the importance of TT activities.

Regulations have an impact on spin-off activity because they determine the degree to which universities have the autonomy to make their own rules regarding TT activities, like the reputation and research eminence of individual universities. Even the institutional factors such as culture of the university, its attitude towards spin-offs and the competence of the technology transfer offices, could have an impact on this phenomenon. Moreover, the distribution of spin-offs across industry sectors is highly uneven and spin-offs are diverse in their activities because they reflect the prevalent sectors of research and activities of universities.

5 Academic Spin-Off as an Innovative Start-Up

The legislation relating to innovative start-ups is regulated by art. 25 of Legislative Decree n. 179/2012, converted by Law no. 221/2012, and its subsequent modifications. The legislation provides a series of requirements for a company to qualify as an innovative start-up.

After this law, the most part of academic spin-offs applied for the registration as innovative start-up to benefit of the incentives that the Italian government wanted to give to knowledge-based firms with the so-called "Decreto Sviluppo".

In this sense, it could be interesting to show the main characteristics of this phenomenon in Italy.

5.1 Definition of Innovative Start-Up

For a clearer identification that does not generate arbitrators, it is necessary to define a series of criteria for these new innovative companies. An innovative start-up is a new company that introduces significant innovation to the market.

This innovation can be a process as well as a product. Indeed, it may concern the products and services offered or new production methods for existing products and services or organizational innovations. As complete as this definition seems, it is actually not easy to evaluate the actual degree of "innovation" of a new business project, especially since at the time of launch, the actual market potential of the new idea is difficult to evaluate. An innovation is not such if it does not demonstrate its value on the market. On the other hand, precisely because of the "novelty" characteristics present in this type of business, the probability of failure is high. For these reasons, it is necessary to adopt more objective criteria, which make it possible to recognize a "potential" innovative start-up even before it has demonstrated its validity on the market. The different definitions adopted in national and EU legislation refer to some parameters that empirical studies have highlighted as characterizing innovative start-ups. These parameters concern, among others, the presence of people with high levels of qualification (degree or doctorate) and the commitment of spending in Research and Development (R&D). The use of these parameters recognizes the fact that in new competitive contexts, innovation is increasingly based on the practical application of scientific knowledge.

The list of requirements is contained in the art. 25 of law and states that:

1. The company has been established for no more than sixty months (a duration considered sufficient for the start-up phase of a new innovative company);
2. the company has the principal place of business and interests in Italy;
3. Starting from the second year of activity of the innovative start-up, the total value of annual production does not exceed 5 million euros, as resulting from the last approved financial statements within six months of the end of the year;
4. the company does not distribute profits. The profits are used to keep the company capitalized or can in any case be reinvested in R&D thus helping the start-up to grow;
5. the company has the development, production and marketing of innovative products or services with high technological value as exclusive or prevalent object;
6. the company was not formed by a merger, company split or following the sale of a company or business unit.

Additionally, at least one of the following requirements is required:

I. Research and Development expenses are equal to or greater than 15% of the higher value between cost and total production value of the innovative start-up. In the absence of financial statements in the first year of life, the legal representative of the innovative start-up will sign a declaration.

II. At least one-third of the total workforce must have a Ph.D. or be a Ph.D. student at an Italian or foreign university, or have a degree and have carried out certified research for at least three years at public or private research institutes, in Italy or abroad, or two-thirds of the overall workforce with a master's degree (art.3, Decree of the Minister of Education, 22 October 2004, n. 270).

III. Is the owner of at least one industrial property right relating to an industrial, biotechnological invention, a topography of semi-conductor products or a new plant variety or is the owner of the rights related to an original computer program registered with the Special Public Register for computer programs, provided that these proprietary rights are directly related to the corporate purpose and business activity.

Start-ups that meet the basic requisite can register in the section dedicated to it in the Register of Companies and benefit from a series of tax breaks, also for the purposes of registering the establishment and registration of the company in the Register of Companies (in particular the art. 26–31 of Legislative Decree no. 179/2012, converted by Law no. 221/2012), derogations from company law and a specific regulation relating to employment relationships in the company.

5.2 *Main Evidence from Italy*

A positive image of the start-up phenomenon in Italy emerges from the first quarter of 2019 report prepared by MISE (Ministry of Economic Development). At the end of the 2nd quarter of 2019, the number of innovative start-ups registered in the special division of the Register of Companies pursuant to Legislative Decree 179/2012 is equal to 10,426, with an increase of 351 units (+3.48%) compared to the end of March 2018.

Among the 361 thousand joint-stock companies established in Italy in the last five years and still in active status, on the date of the survey of MISE (1 July 2019), 2.88% of them were registered as an innovative start-up, an increase compared to 2.82% recorded in the previous quarter (1st quarter 2019). As regards the breakdown by business sector, 73.1% of innovative start-ups provide services to businesses (with a prevalence, in particular, of the following specializations: software production and IT consultancy, 34.6%; R&D activities, 13.7%; information service activities, 9.2%), 18.1% work in manufacturing activities (especially machinery manufacturing for 3.2%; manufacture of computers and electronic and optical products for 2.9%), while 3.5% operate in commerce. In many economic sectors, the weight of innovative start-ups out of the total of new joint-stock companies appears considerable. 8.1% of the companies appear to be an innovative start-up operating in the business services sector; for manufacturing, the corresponding percentage is 4.9%. In some sectors, the presence of innovative companies is particularly high: 35.3% of new companies with code C26 (computer manufacturing), 36.2% of those with code J62 (software production) are an innovative start-up, and even 68.2% of those with the M72 code (Research and Development).

Looking at the composition of the company structure, there are 1412 innovative start-ups with a female preponderance, or in which the majority of the shares and administrative offices are held by women, 13.5% of the total: a significantly lower incidence than the 22% observed taking into consideration the universe of new joint-stock companies. There are 4499 innovative start-ups in which at least one woman is present in the company structure, 43.2% of the total: a lower share, even if to a lesser extent, than that found in the other new joint-stock companies (47.3%). There are 2014 innovative youth start-uppers (under 35), 19.3% of the total. There are 347 innovative start-ups with a foreign-owned company, 3.3% of the total, a smaller share than that of the other new joint-stock companies (8.6%). On the other hand, 13.7% (1424) are the innovative start-ups in which at least one component is not an Italian citizen, a ratio more similar to that found among limited companies (14.7%).

By examining the geographical distribution of the phenomenon, Lombardy remains the region in which the largest number of innovative start-ups are situated: 2656, equal to 25.5% of the national total. It is followed by Lazio, the only other region to exceed one thousand (1156; 11.1%), and Emilia-Romagna (903, 8.7% of the national total). In a short distance, Veneto appears in fourth place, with 890 start-ups (8.5%), followed by Campania, largely the first region of the South with 818 (7.9%). In the queue appear Basilicata with 111, Molise with 75, and Valle d'Aosta with 22 innovative start-ups. Milan is by far the province where the highest number of innovative start-ups are located: in mid-2019 they were 1860, equal to 17.8% of the national total. Rome ranks 2nd, the only other province to exceed 1000 (1012 start-ups, 10% of the national total). All the other major provinces are characterized by values that are very distant from those in the top positions: the top 5 includes, in order, Naples (380, 3.6%), Turin (338, 3.2%) and Bologna (322, 3.1%). The top 10 is completed by Padua, Bari, Verona, Salerno, Trento and Bergamo.

In terms of employment, at the end of March 2019 there were 3918 innovative start-ups with at least one employee (353 less than at the end of December). The innovative start-ups are characterized by significantly larger companies than the other new joint-stock companies: on average, each start-up has 4.5 partners, as opposed to the 2.1 established among the other comparable new companies. On 31 March 2019, the global figure of shareholders and employees involved in start-up activities reaches 59,103. In the first quarter of the current year, the workforce increased by 4345 units, while the year-over-year increase was 10,138 units (+20.7%).

Finally, coming to the economic and financial indicators, data on the median production value is equal to 27,635 euro, a significantly lower value than the average: further proof of the fact that most of the innovative start-ups listed are still in an embryonic condition of development. The total operating income recorded in 2017 is around 81 million euros.

As is physiological for companies with high technological content that have longer market access times, the incidence of companies at a loss among innovative start-ups is significantly higher than that detectable among non-innovative companies, which however equal 33.8%. The ROI and ROE profitability indicators of innovative start-ups record negative values; if, however, reference is only made for those in profit, the indices are appreciably better than those of the other joint-stock companies (ROI: 0.12 versus 0.05; ROE: 0.27 versus 0.13) (MISE, 2019).

Figure 9 reports the number of innovative star-ups by Region, while Fig. 10 shows the distribution in Italy.

Position	Region	n° of innovative start-ups (2019)	% innovative start-ups/total firms	% innovative start-ups/total capital company
1	Lombardia	2656	25,47	3,95
2	Lazio	1156	11,09	2,25
3	Emilia-Romagna	903	8,66	3,51
4	Veneto	890	8,54	3,28
5	Campania	818	7,85	2,01
6	Piemonte	552	5,29	3,11
7	Sicilia	517	4,96	2,24
8	Toscana	441	4,23	1,93
9	Puglia	414	3,97	1,81
10	Marche	375	3,60	4,03
11	Trentino-Alto Adige	271	2,60	5,46
12	Calabria	231	2,22	2,48
13	Abruzzo	226	2,17	2,57
14	Friuli-Venezia Giulia	223	2,14	4,75
15	Umbria	199	1,91	3,98
16	Ligura	196	1,88	2,91
17	Sardegna	150	1,44	1,83
18	Basilicata	111	1,06	3,42
19	Molise	75	0,72	3,63
20	Valle d'Aosta	22	0,21	5,26

Fig. 9 Number of innovative start-ups by Italian regions (*Sources* Author's elaboration on MISE report, 2019)

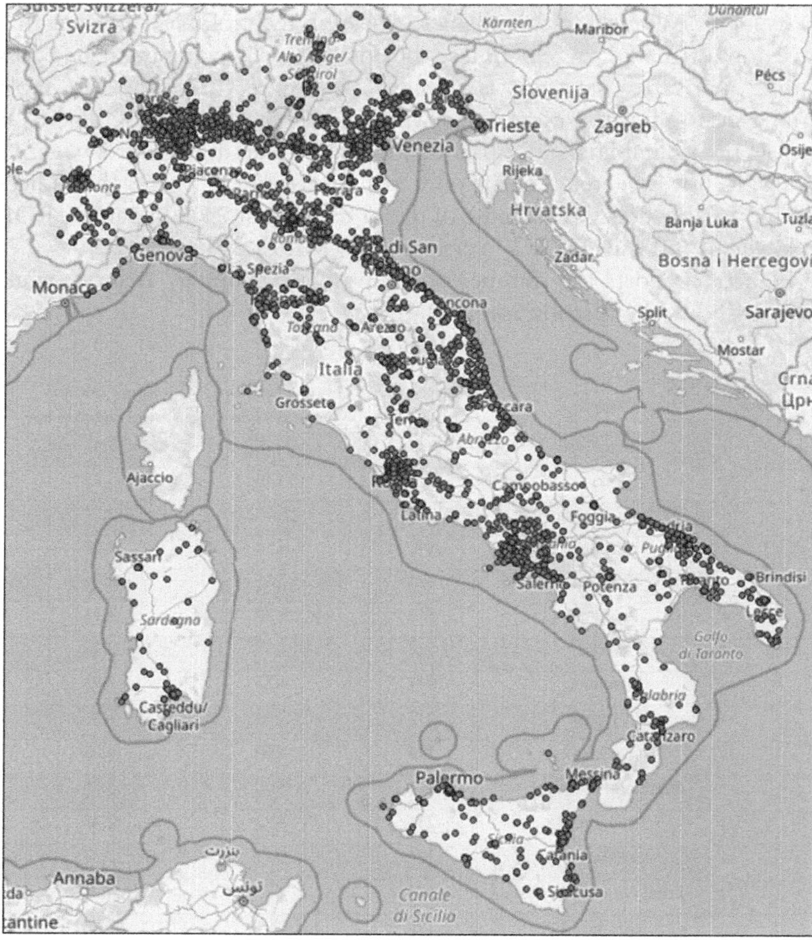

Fig. 10 Distribution of innovative start-up in Italy (*Sources* Carloni et al., 2020)

6 Conclusion

The increased emphasis on transferring technology from academia to the private sector for commercialization as an economic development strategy has led to a rise in entrepreneurial activities in universities. As a consequence, studies on university technology transfer increase and scholars star to analyse the convergence and contrast of scientific and commercial opportunities for researchers.

Academic scientists participate in a wide spectrum of entrepreneurial behaviours and their choices are influenced by university organizational mechanisms and public policies that can foster or prevent the technology transfer.

Any scientist, whose shelves are full of prototypes and proofs of concepts awaiting commercial developed, is a potential academic entrepreneur, who simply lacks adequate economic incentives and/or work in a "Ivory Tower" where the technology transfer from academia to industry is not encouraged.

In order to straighten up the incentives, the policymakers are called to establish clear norms to exploit the results of academic research. Spin-offs is a way to do this and to bring those inventions down from the academic shelves.

According to the Resources Based View, the factors that impede the formation and growth of spin-offs are several and could be lack of competency in founding teams and scarcity of resources. The letter lack refers to inadequate funding and inadequate structural support, while cultural problems are linked to an unsupportive university culture towards spin-offs.

Due to the fact that academic spin-offs could be beneficial to national, regional and local economies, in second chapter, I try to analyse the phenomenon of spin-offs in Italy, investigating the characteristics and the factors affecting the birth and the development of these companies.

Analysing the factors that foster this phenomenon is important because, regardless of the marginal quantitative impact, the spin-offs could have a qualitative impact on local context where they are localized. From this point of view, spin-offs can be important drivers of regional economic development because they generate hi-tech entrepreneurship and represent a connection for other firms to access the expertise and skills within universities, encouraging the development of networks through which new technologies and knowledge can be shared. Academic spin-offs represent a significant example of network between research centres and small firms.

This network allows small firms to build up the technological environment that sustains their innovative capabilities. Furthermore, they are companies in high-tech sectors, so they can contribute to production specialization to knowledge-based activities, and this can improve the quality of regional innovation environment.

The fact that companies founded by academic personnel were likely to locate around universities is a somehow desirable feature from the point of view of policymakers, concerned on fostering economic development locally.

Policies to foster this phenomenon have to take into account these considerations, stimulating entrepreneurial spirit and knowledge spin-off in public research because they are a good way in which radical technologies can be transferred to society.

The PRI can play a decisive role in supporting spin-offs, first of all by promoting a climate which is favourable and supportive for the new high-tech ventures. Indeed, this form of technology transfer requires a strong supportive infrastructure and sufficient entrepreneurial human capital, so University can support spin-offs with Business incubators and the offices responsible for technology transfer (Industrial Liaison Office). They are key tools for transferring expertise and resources from research to production activities and for promoting the start-up and early development of spin-offs.

At this level, the possible support services could be:

- scouting and generation of business ideas in the academic environment;
- support in preparing a business plan to verify the real market potential;
- assistance in raising capital and trading partners.

An incubator could facilitate the learning processes among the founders and it helps founders overcome their inexperience of the business development process and their limited understanding of the context in which the business seeks to establish itself. Both of these activities help founders to overcome the liabilities of newness and facilitate the commercialization of business proposals.

In addition to these areas of intervention, the study on a sample of Italian spin-offs highlighted the need to pay more attention to evaluating the entrepreneurial team that promotes the spin-off.

This could help developers to gain greater insight into the objectives underlying the establishment of spin-offs and to consider the possibility of integrating the entrepreneurial team when starting up the new initiative.

Last but not least, PRI can support academic spin-offs contributing to the development and training of resources and skills to bridge the knowledge gaps highlighted by the survey: gaps related to business culture and management and gaps related to the commercialization of the new technologies. Entrepreneurial education for nascent academic entrepreneurs could play a fundamental role in this direction. The explosion of interest for the entrepreneurship field has resulted also in the institution of courses and degrees at undergraduate and graduate level. Courses about entrepreneurship have grown steadily in all the main countries.

In this context, the Italian situation is rather "anomalous" as entrepreneurship education at the university level is still at an embryonic stage. This seems in vivid contrast with the need for Italy to foster the formation of new firms.

Compared with the situation observed in the US and in other European countries, entrepreneurship education is Italy is rather "underdeveloped". Only a few of Italian universities have courses dedicated to entrepreneurship. The courses are concentrated within business faculties while very few exist in engineering faculties. Moreover, in most cases the courses deal with the development of the business plan and are offered as a way to support the participation of students and researchers to start-up competitions rather than as part of official curricula. The courses are generally run by external teachers on the basis of temporary contracts rather than by tenured professors. This situation contrasts with the potential importance of entrepreneurship education at the university level in the Italian case. In fact, the spread of entrepreneurship courses could contribute to reducing some of the weaknesses of the Italian entrepreneurship model, as highlighted by the results of the empirical analysis carried out in the two chapters of this book: (a) new businesses are concentrated in traditional sectors while there are too few start-ups in high-tech sectors; (b) academic spin-offs that, by definition, are high-tech firms tend to remain small, rather than pursuing rapid growth for several reasons, one of them is the lack in managerial competences of team of promoters.

The slow pace with which Italian universities are keeping up with the global trend in entrepreneurship education at the university level could depend on two main factors, both referring to the supply side. On the one hand, the presence of a cultural tradition that favours theoretical rather than practical education. On the other hand, there are some rigidities of the Italian university system that do not favour the introduction of new research disciplines or research fields that, like entrepreneurship, have an interdisciplinary nature (Iacobucci & Micozzi, 2012).

Bibliography

Acosta, M., Coronado, D., & Flores, E. (2011). University spillovers and new business location in high-technology sectors: Spanish evidence. *Small Business Economics, 36*(3), 365–376.

Acs, Z., Desai, S., & Hessels, J. (2008). Entrepreneurship, economic development and institutions. *Small Business Economics, 31*(3), 219–234.

Argote, L., & Ingram, P. (2000). Knowledge transfer: A basis for competitive advantage in firms. *Organizational Behavior and Human Decision Processes, 82*(1), 150–169.

Åstebroa, T., Bazzaziana, N., & Braguinskyb, S. (2012). Startups by recent university graduates and their faculty: Implications for university entrepreneurship policy. *Research Policy, 41*, 663–667.

Audretsch, D. B. (2012). From the entrepreneurial university to the university for the entrepreneurial society. *The Journal of Technology Transfer, 39*(3), 313–321.

Audretsch, D. B., & Feldman, M. P. (1996). R&D spillovers and the geography of innovation and production. *American Economic Review, 86*, 630–640.

Audretsch, D. B., & Stephan, P. E. (1999). Knowledge spillovers in biotechnology: Sources and incentives. *Journal of Evolutionary Economics, 9*(1), 97–107.

Audretsch, D. B., & Vivarelli, M. (1996). Firms size and R&D spillovers: Evidence from Italy. *Small Business Economics, 8*(3), 225–237.

Audretsch, D. B., Keilbach, M. C., & Lehmann, E. E. (2006). *Entrepreneurship and Economic Growth*. New York: Oxford University Press.

Bammer, G. (2008). Enhancing research collaborations: Three key management challenges. *Research Policy, 37*(5), 875–887.

Barbieri, E., Rubini, L., Pollio, C., & Micozzi, A. (2018). What are the trade-offs of academic entrepreneurship? An investigation on the Italian case. *Journal of Technology Transfer, 43*(1), 198–221.

Ben-Hafaïedh, C., Micozzi, A., & Pattitoni, P. (2018). Academic spin-offs' entrepreneurial teams and performance: A subgroups approach. *Journal of Technology Transfer, 43*(3), 714–733.

Berbegal-Mirabent, J., Ribeiro-Soriano, D. E., & Sánchez García, J. L. (2015). Can a magic recipe foster university spin-off creation? *Journal of Business Research, 68*(11), 2272–2278.

Bercovitz, J., & Feldmann, M. (2006). Entrepreneurial universities and technology transfer: A conceptual framework for understanding knowledge-based economic development. *Journal of Technology Transfer, 31*(1), 175–188.

Birley, S. (1985). The role of networks in the entrepreneurial process. *Journal of Business Venturing* (Vol. 1, pp. 107–117).

Blanchflower, D. G., Oswald, A., & Stutzer, A. (2001). Latent entrepreneurship across nations. *European Economic Review, 45*(4–6), 680–691.

Bonaccorsi, A., & Daraio, C. (2005). Exploring size and agglomeration effects on public research productivity. *Scientometrics, 63*(1), 87–120.

Bonardo, D., Paleari, S., & Vismara, S. (2011). Valuing university-based firms: The effects of academic affiliation on IPO performance. *Entrepreneurship: Theory and Practice, 35*(4), 755–776.

Bonte, W., Falck, O., & Heblich, S. (2009). The impact of regional age structure on entrepreneurship. *Economic Geography, 83*(3), 269–287.

Boucher, G., Conway, C., & van der Meer, E. (2003). Tiers of engagement by university in their regions development. *Regional Studies, 37*(9), 887–897.

Bradley, S. R., Hayter, C. S., & Link, A. N. (2013). Models and methods of university technology transfer. *Foundations and Trends® in Entrepreneurship, 9*(6), 571–650.

Budyldina, N. (2018). Entrepreneurial universities and regional contribution. *International Entrepreneurship and Management Journal, 14*(2), 265–277.

Carayannis, E. G., & Campbell, D. F. J. (2010). Triple Helix, Quadruple Helix and Quintuple Helix, and how do knowledge, innovation and the environment relate to each other? A proposed framework for a trans-disciplinary analysis of sustainable development and social ecology. *International Journal of Social Ecology and Sustainable Development, 1*(1), 41–69.

Carloni, M., Ciarrocchi, A., & Micozzi, A. (2020). La vicinanza all'Università? Un'opportunità. Le scelte di localizzazione delle start-up innovative italiane. *L'Industria, XLI*(4), 81–102.

Cesaroni, F., & Piccaluga, A. (2005). Universities and intellectual property rights in Southern European countries. *Technology Analysis Strategic Management, 17*(4), 497–518.

Cesaroni, F., & Piccaluga, A. (2015). The activities of university knowledge transfer offices: Towards the third mission in Italy. *The Journal of Technology Transfer, 41*(4), 753–777.

Chesbrough, H. W. (2003). Open innovation: The new imperative for creating and profiting from technology. *Perspectives Academy of Management* (Vol. 20). Harvard Business Press.

Chiesa, V., & Piccaluga, A. (2000). Exploitation and diffusion of public research: The case of academic spin-off companies in Italy. *R and D Management, 30*(4), 329–340.

Clarysse, B., & Moray, N. (2004). A process study of entrepreneurial team formation: The case of a research-based spin-off. *Journal of Business Venturing, 19*(1), 55–79.

Clarysse, B., Wright, M., Lockett, A., Mustar, P., & Knockaert, M. (2007). Academic spin-offs, formal technology transfer and capital raising. *Industrial and Corporate Change, 16*(4), 609–640.

Colombo, M. G., & Piva, E. (2008). Strengths and weaknesses of academic startups: A conceptual model. *IEEE Transactions on Engineering Management, 55*(1), 37–49.

Cooke, P., Heidenreich, M., & Braczyk, H. (2004). *Regional innovation systems.* London: Routledge.

Cooper, A. C., & Bruno, A. V. (1977). Success among high-technology firms. *Business Horizons, 20*(2), 16–22.

Czarnitzki, D., Rammer, C., & Toole, A. A. (2014). University spin-offs and the '"performance premium"'. *Small Business Economics, 43,* 309–326.

Dacin, T. (1997). Isomorphism in context: The power and prescriptions of institutional norms. *Academy and Management Journal, 40*(1), 46–81.

Dahlstrand, A. L. (1999). Technology-based SMEs in the Goteborg region: Their origin and interaction with universities and large firms. *Regional Studies, 33*(4), 379–389.

De Turi, I., & Garzoni, A. (2018). The impact of the external environment on the growth of the italian academic spin-offs: A cross-sectional analysis. *International Journal of Business and Management, 13*(8), 16–25.

Delmar, F., Davidsson, P., & Gartner, W. B. (2003). Arriving at the high-growth firm. *Journal of Business Venturing, 18*(2), 189–216.

D'Este, P. D., Mahdi, S., & Neely, A. (2010). *Academic entrepreneurship: What are the factors shaping the capacity of academic researchers to identify and exploit entrepreneurial opportunities?* (DRUID Working Papers, No. 10). DRUID, Copenhagen Business School, Department of Industrial Economics and Strategy/Aalborg University, Department of Business Studies.

Denis, J. L., & Lomas, J. (2003). Convergent evolution: The academic and policy roots of collaborative research. *Journal of Health Services Research & Policy, 8*(2), 1–6.

Di Gregorio, D., & Shane, S. (2003). Why do some universities generate more start-ups than others? *Research Policy, 32*(2), 209–227.

Ding, W. W. (2011). The impact of founders' professional-education background on the adoption of open science by for-profit biotechnology firms. *Management Science, 57*(2), 257–273.

Djokovic, D., & Souitaris, V. (2008). Spinouts from academic institutions: A literature review with suggestions for further research. *The Journal of Technology Transfer, 33*(3), 225–247.

Druilhe, C., & Garnsey, E. (2004). Do academic spin-outs differ and does it matter? *The Journal of Technology Transfer, 29*(3), 269–285.

Etzkowitz, H. (1983). Entrepreneurial scientists and entrepreneurial universities in American academic science. *Minerva, 21*(2–3), 198–233.

Etzkowitz, H. (2003). Innovation in innovation: The triple helix of university-industry-government relations. *Social Science Information, 42*(3), 293–337.

Etzkowitz, H., & Leydesdorff, L. (2000). The dynamics of innovation: From National Systems and '"Mode 2"' to a Triple Helix of university–industry–government relations. *Science and Technology, 29*(2), 109–123.

Etzkowitz, H., Webster, A., Gebhardt, C., & Terra, B. R. C. (2000). The future of the university and the university of the future: Evolution of ivory tower to entrepreneurial paradigm. *Research Policy, 29*(2), 313–330.

Ferretti, M., Ferri, S., Fiorentino, R., Parmentola, A., & Sapio, A. (2019). Neither absent nor too present: The effects of the engagement of parent universities on the performance of academic spin-offs. *Small Business Economics, 52,* 153–173.

Ferri, S., & Fiorentino, R. (2019). Patenting or not? The dilemma of academic spin-off founders. *Business Process Management Journal, 25*(1), 84–103.

Fini, R., Fu, K., Mathisen, M. T., Rasmussen, E., & Wright, M. (2017). Institutional determinants of university spin-off quantity and quality: A longitudinal, multilevel, cross-country study. *Small Business Economics, 48*(2), 361–391.

Franzoni, C., & Lissoni, F. (2009). Academic entrepreneurship: Definitional issues, policy implications and a research agenda. In A. Varga (Ed.), *Academic entrepreneurship and regional development*. London: Edward Elgar.

Galunic, D. C., & Rodan, S. (1998). Resource recombinations in the firm: Knowledge structures and the potential for schumpeterian innovation. *Strategic Management Journal, 19*(12), 1193–1201.

Gibbons, M., Limoges, C., Nowotny, H., Schwartzman, S., Scott, P., & Trow, M. (1994). *The new production of knowledge: The dynamics of science and research in contemporary societies* (M. Gibbons, Ed.), *Information processing & management* (Vol. 31). London: Sage.

Heirman, A., & Clarysse, B. (2004). How and why do research-based start-ups differ at founding? A resource-based configurational perspective. *The Journal of Technology Transfer, 29*(3/4), 247–268.

Hewitt-Dundas, N. (2013). The role of proximity in university-business cooperation for innovation. *The Journal of Technology Transfer, 38,* 93–115.

Heydebreck, P., Klofsten, M., & Maier, J. C. (2000). Innovation support for new technology based firms: The Swedish Teknopol approch. *R&D Management, 30*(1), 89–100.

Hoang, H., & Antoncic, B. (2003). Network-based research in entrepreneurship. *Journal of Business Venturing, 18*(2), 165–187.

Iacobucci, D., Iacopini, A., Micozzi, A., & Orsini, S. (2011). Fostering entrepreneurship in academic spin-offs. *International Journal of Entrepreneurship and Small Business, 12*(4), 513–533.

Iacobucci, D., & Micozzi, A. (2012). Entrepreneurship education in Italian universities: Trend, situation and opportunities. *Education and Training, 54*(8/9), 673–696.

Iacobucci, D., & Micozzi, A. (2015). How to evaluate the impact of academic spin-offs on local development: An empirical analysis of the Italian case. *Journal of Technology Transfer, 40*(3), 434–452.

Jacobsson, S., & Rickne, A. (2004). How large is the Swedish 'academic' sector really? A critical analysis of the use of science and technology indicators. *Research Policy, 33*(9), 1355–1372.

Johansson, M., Jacob, M., & Hellström, T. (2005). The Strength of Strong Ties: University Spin-offs and the Significance of Historical Relations. *The Journal of Technology Transfer, 30*(3), 271–286.

Judge, T. A., Cable, D. M., Colbert, A. E., & Rynes, S. L. (2007). What causes a management article to be cited-article, author, or journal? *Academy of Management Journal, 50,* 491–506.

Karlsson, T., & Wigren, C. (2012). Start-ups among university employees: The influence of legitimacy, human capital and social capital. *The Journal of Technology Transfer, 37,* 297–312.

Kostova, T., & Roth, K. (2003). Social capital in multinational corporation and a micro-macro model of its formation. *Academy of Management Review, 28,* 297–317.

Landry, R., Amara, N., & Rherrad, I. (2006). Why are some university researchers more likely to create spin-offs than others? *Evidence from Canadian Universities. Research Policy, 35*(10), 1599–1615.

Lawton Smith, H., & Ho, K. (2006). Measuring the performance of Oxford university, Oxford Brookes university and the government laboratories' spin-off companies. *Research Policy, 35,* 1554–1568.

Lazzeri, F., & Piccaluga, A. (2012). Le imprese spin-off della ricerca pubblica: Convinzioni, realtà e prospettive future. *Economia E Società Regionale, 1,* 43–65.

Leitch, C. M., & Harrison, R. T. (2005). Maximising the potential of university spin-outs: The development of second-order commercialisation activities. *R&D Management, 35*(3), 257–272.

Leitch, C. M., & Harrison, R. T. (2010). Voodoo institution or entrepreneurial university? Spin-off companies, the entrepreneurial system and regional development in the Uk. *Regional Studies, 44*(9), 1241–1262.

Lissoni, F. (2010). Academic inventors as brokers. *Research Policy, 39*(7), 843–857.

Locke, E. A. (1976). The nature and causes of job satisfaction. In M. D. Dunnette (Ed.), *Handbook of industrial and organizational psychology* (Vol. 1, pp. 1297–1349). Chicago: Rand McNally.

Lockett, A., & Wright, M. (2005). Resources, capabilities, risk capital and the creation of university spin-out companies. *Research Policy, 34*(7), 1043–1057.

Lockett, A., Wright, M., & Franklin, S. (2003). Technology transfer and universities' spin-out strategies. *Small Business Economics, 20,* 185–201.

Louis, K. S., Blumenthal, D., Gluck, M. E., & Stoto, M. A. (1989). Entrepreneurs in academe: An exploration of behaviors among life scientists. *Administrative Science Quarterly, 34*(1), 110–131. https://doi.org/10.2307/2392988.

Lowe, R. A. (2001). *Entrepreneurship and information asymmetry: Theory and evidence from the University of California-Berkeley*. Citeseer.

Martelli, I., Micozzi, A., Iacobucci, D., & Piccaluga, A. (2019). *Engines need belt transmissions: The importance of people in Technology Transfer Offices* (Working Paper Netval n.1/19).

Mathieu, A. (2011). *University-industry interactions and knowledge transfer mechanisms: A critical survey* (Working Papers CEB). *Zucker* (Vol. 32).

Meoli, M., & Vismara, S. (2016). University support and the creation of technology and non-technology academic spin-offs. *Small Business Economics, 47*(2), 345–362.

MISE. (2019). *Rapporto 2o trimestre 2019 – cruscotto di indicatori statistici sulle start-up innovative*. Roma.

Muscio, A., Quaglione, D., & Ramaciotti, L. (2016). The effects of university rules on spinoff creation: The case of academia in Italy. *Research Policy, 45*(7), 1386–1396.

Mustar, P. (1997). How French academics create hi-tech companies: The conditions for success or failure. *Science and Public Policy, 24*(1), 37–44.

Mustar, P., & Wright, M. (2010). Convergence or path dependency in policies to foster the creation of university spin-off firms? A comparison of France and the United Kingdom. *The Journal of Technology Transfer, 35,* 42–65.

Nicolaou, N., & Birley, S. (2003). Academic networks in a trichotomous categorisation of university spinouts. *Journal of Business Venturing, 18*(3), 333–359.

OECD. (2005). Science, Technology and Industry. *Scoreboard 2005.* Paris: OECD Publishing.

Oliver, A. L. (2004). Biotechnology entrepreneurial scientists and their collaborations. *Research Policy, 33*(4), 583–597. https://doi.org/10.1016/j.respol.2004.01.010.

O'Shea, R., Chugh, H., & Allen, T. (2007). Determinants and consequences of university spinoff activity: A conceptual framework. *The Journal of Technology Transfer, 33*, 653–666.

Pavitt, K. (1984). Sectoral patterns of technical change: Towards a taxonomy and a theory. *Research Policy, 13*, 343–373.

Penrose, E. (1959). *The theory of the growth of the firm*. Oxford: Basil Blackwell.

Piccaluga, A., Balderi, C., & Patrono, A. (n.d.). *Le imprese spin-off della ricerca pubblica in Italia*.

Poma, L., & Ramaciotti, L. (2008). La valorizzazione della ricerca universitaria mediante l'interpolazione dei saperi. Infrastrutture materiali e immateriali. *L'Industria, XXIX*(Numero speciale), 269–297.

Porter, M. (1980). *Competitive strategy: Tecniques for analyzing industries and competitors*. New York: The Free Press.

Powers, J. B., & McDougall, P. P. (2005). University start-up formation and technology licensing with firms that go public: A resource-based view of academic entrepreneurship. *Journal of Business Venturing, 20*(3), 291–311.

Radosevich, R. (1995). A model for entrepreneurial spin-offs from public technology sources. *International Journal of Technology Management, 10*(7–8), 879–893.

Ramaciotti, L., & Daniele, C. (2018). *La rete del trasferimento tecnologico si rafforza con la clinical innovation*. Pisa.

Rasmussen, E., Mosey, S., & Wright, M. (2011). The evolution of entrepreneurial competencies: A longitudinal study of university spin-off venture emergence. *Journal of Management Studies, 48*(6), 1314–1345.

Roberts, E. B. (1991). High stakes for high-tech entrepreneurs: Understanding venture capital decision making. *Sloan Management Review, 32*(2), 9–20.

Rodríguez-Navarro, A., & Narin, F. (2018). European paradox or delusion—Are European science and economy outdated? *Science and Public Policy, 45*(1), 14–23.

Rogers, E. M., Takegami, S., & Yin, J. (2001). Lessons learned about technology transfer. *Technovation, 21*(4), 253–261.

Romer, P. (1990). Endogenous technological change. *Journal of Political Economy, 98*(5), S71–S102.

Rothaermel, F. T., Agung, S. D., & Jiang, L. (2007). University entrepreneurship: A taxonomy of the literature. *Industrial and Corporate Change, 16*(4), 691–791.

Scholten, V., Omta, O., Kemp, R., & Elfring, T. (2015). Bridging ties and the role of research and start-up experience on the early growth of Dutch academic spin-offs. *Technovation, 45–46*, 40–51.

Shane, S. (2000). Prior knowledge and the discovery of entrepreneurial opportunities. *Organization Science, 11*(4), 448–469. https://doi.org/10.1287/orsc.11.4.448.14602.

Shane, S. (2001). Technological opportunities and new firm creation. *Management Science, 47*(2), 205–220.

Shane, S. (2002). Executive Forum: University technology transfer to entrepreneurial companies. *Journal of Business Venturing, 17*(6), 537–552.

Shane, S. (2004). Encouraging university entrepreneurship? The effect of the Bayh-Dole Act on university patenting in the United States. *Journal of Business Venturing, 19*(1), 127–151.

Shane, S., & Stuart, T. (2002). Organizational endowments and the performance of university start-ups. *Management Science, 48*(1), 154–170.

Siegel, D. S., Waldman, D., & Link, A. (1999). *Assessing the impact of organizational practices on the productivity of university technology transfer offices: An exploratory study. national bureau of economic research working paper series* (Vol. No. 7256). National Bureau of Economic Research Cambridge, MA, USA.

Siegel, D. S., & Wright, M. (2015). University technology transfer offices, licensing and start-ups. In N. Link, D. S. Siegel, & M. Wright (Eds.), *The Chicago handbook of university technology transfer and academic entrepreneurship* (pp. 1–40). Chicago: Chicago University Press.

Smilor, R. W., & Matthews, J. (2004). University venturing: Technology transfer and commercialisation in higher education. *International Journal Technological Transfer Commercial, 3*(1), 111–128.

Soetanto, D. P. (2009). Socioeconomic networks: In search of better support for university spin-offs. In R. Oakey, A. Groen, G. Cook, & P. van Der Sijde (Eds.), *New technology-based firms in the new millennium* (pp. 165–184). Bingley: Emerald Group Publishing Limited.

Stephan, P. E., & Levin, S. G. (1996). Property rights and entrepreneurship in science. *Small Business Economics, 8*(3), 177–188.

Stuart, T. E., & Ding, W. W. (2006). When do scientists become entrepreneurs? The social structural antecedents of commercial activity in the academic life sciences. *AJS the University of Chicago, 112*(1), 97–144.

Ucbasaran, D., Westhead, P., & Wright, M. (2007). Opportunity Identification and pursuit: Does an entrepreneur's human capital matter? *Small Business Economics, 30*(2), 153–173.

Van Stel, A., Carree, M., & Thurik, R. (2005). The effect of entrepreneurial activity on national economic growth. *Small Business Economics, 24*(3), 311–321.

Vanaelst, I., Clarysse, B., Wright, M., Lockett, A., Moray, N., & S'Jegers, R. (2006). Entrepreneurial team development in academic spinouts: An examination of team heterogeneity. *Entrepreneurship Theory and Practice, 30*(2), 249–271.

Varga, A. (2006). The spatial dimension of innovation and growth: Empirical research methodology and policy analysis. *European Planning Studies, 14*(9), 1171–1186.

Vohara, A., Wright, M., & Lockett, A. (2004). Critical junctures in the development of university high-tech spinout companies. *Research Policy, 3*(1), 147–175.

Wiklund, J., & Shepherd, D. (2003). Knowledge-based resources, entrepreneurial orientation, and the performance of small and medium-sized businesses. *Strategic Management Journal, 24*(13), 1307–1314.

Wright, M., Clarysse, B., Lockett, A., & Knockaert, M. (2008). Mid-range universities' linkages with industry: Knowledge types and the role of intermediaries. *Research Policy, 37*(8), 1205–1223.

Wright, M., Lockett, A., Clarysse, B., & Binks, M. (2006). University spin-out companies and venture capital. *Research Policy, 35*, 481–501.

Yli-Renko, H., Autio, E., & Sapienza, H. J. (2001). Social capital, knowledge acquisition, and knowledge exploitation in young technology-based firms. *Strategic Management Journal, 22*(6–7), 587–613.

Ziman, J. (1994). *Prometheus bound: Science in a dynamic steady state*. New York: Cambridge University Press.

CHAPTER 3

Concluding Remarks

Abstract The last chapter of this book provides some conclusions and policy implications, highlighting an important aspect: the role of education in the creation of a solid entrepreneurial culture among citizens.

Keywords Knowledge spillover · University · Technology transfer

1 Introduction

The book presents two chapters on entrepreneurship: the first one analyses the process for setting up new initiatives, investigating several factors related to entrepreneurship dynamic, the second one focuses on a type of high-tech entrepreneurship, the academic entrepreneurship, investigating in depth the phenomenon of academic spin-offs.

Specifically, the most important evidence of the first chapter is that Italy reports the lowest index of entrepreneurial dynamics in the global ranking, according to the GEM consortium and the lowest share of new high-tech firms in a comparison with EU countries.

In this sense it is important to understand the reasons affecting these worrying results to suggest policy actions fostering entrepreneurship, in particular high-tech entrepreneurship.

A. Micozzi, *The Entrepreneurial Dynamics in Italy*,
https://doi.org/10.1007/978-3-030-55183-4_3

2 From Neoclassical Growth Theory to Knowledge Spillover Theory of Entrepreneurship

According to the literature, while the neoclassical growth theory considered economic growth as a process of mere accumulation of production capital, the endogenous growth theory, adopted in this book, shifted the lens to the importance of knowledge in the production process and its potential to create spillovers. The gap between knowledge and exploitable knowledge or economic knowledge should be closed by nascent entrepreneurs who recognize the opportunity enclosed inside knowledge spillovers.

In this framework, technological innovation is seen as the most important factor for achieving long-term economic growth. In advanced countries growth is powered by the capacity of nascent entrepreneurs to innovate by competing in new global markets with their technologically advanced products.

The rise of the modern economy has changed the coordination and cooperation between the main actors involved in the economy, particularly in relation to diffusing, using and exploiting knowledge.

It is increasingly recognized that when a country wants to prosper within the knowledge economy, a strong integration of industry, universities and institutions is required in the areas of science and technology.

Universities play a new role in this process. Traditionally the primary goal of universities lies in the advancement of scientific research and education. These goals make universities a unique source of basic and applied research that can function as an important source of knowledge-based economic growth.

Universities are gradually becoming more involved in economic and social development, and pay more attention to the commercialization of research results, patent and licensing activities, adding entrepreneurial objectives as a third component to their mission. As a result, universities have become more proactive in ensuring the commercialization of their research to help sustain economic growth in the modern economy.

In the second chapter, I investigate one of technology transfer mechanism: the academic spin-offs. Analysing the phenomenon in Italy, the first evidence is that, from a quantitative point of view measurable through turnover or employment, the impact of these firms is rather marginal:

most university spin-offs start small and remain small, reflecting founder aspirations, capabilities and resource endowments.

Three issues might explain this evidence: firstly, knowledge and cultural barriers can occur in the transfer of university knowledge to the business sector, secondly, the imbalance of promoters' skills through technical competences and, thirdly, a lack of entrepreneurial climate might prevent new business creation based on university knowledge.

To evaluate the effective impact of academic spin-offs a change of prospective is needed: starting from the fact that knowledge spillover tends to occur only within limited geographic areas, embedding economic activity based on this knowledge within a local context, the impact of academic spin-off must be evaluated at local level.

University spin-offs should become central to research and innovation policy in Italy because they represent at the same time both one kind of innovative start-up and one kind of technology transfer mechanism. Regional government and economic development institutions, such as Provinces, Chamber of Commerce or development agencies should foster academic entrepreneurship for the potentiality of this phenomenon: the analysis of impact of academic spin-offs at the local level shows that it could be high in terms of creation of hi-tech entrepreneurship and employment and in terms of diffusion of technological spillover.

At a national level, the empirical findings of entrepreneurial dynamics in Italy suggest that the policy actions should be different on the basis of stages of economic development of a local context. For example, in some provinces in Italy, governments should establish confidence in property rights, promote education, safeguard stable macro-economic conditions, make sure that the necessary physical infrastructure is in place and foster female entrepreneurship. Although women have significantly increased their participation in entrepreneurial activities in recent years, the gender gap in firm formation still remains in most parts of the world. Factors that affect this gap include both formal institutions (i.e. childcare facilities) and informal institutions (i.e. traditional role models, religion, family values, the cultural view for which entrepreneurship is perceived as a masculine activity). Starting from the importance of entrepreneurship, female entrepreneurship could be one unexploited source of new firms. Women who set up new ventures introduce variety into the market and, according to the literature, in general, the diversity of economic actors is an essential driver of economic progress at the level of local economies (van der Zwan, Verheul, & Thurik, 2012).

For the economically most advanced local context, the policy actions should be fostering investment in research and development, improving the incentives for self-employment, promoting the commercial exploitation of scientific findings also encouraging a well-developed market for venture capital and stimulating entrepreneurship education and training.

Developing an entrepreneurial culture should start with developing awareness. Everyone should know the importance of entrepreneurs for society, but the subsequent step is to stimulate a positive attitude towards entrepreneurship and develop entrepreneurial qualities such as risk-taking, creativity, initiative and goal setting. The last step is to teach entrepreneurial skills, such as management skills, business plan development, and to experience entrepreneurship hands-on. In Italy, there is a lack of an integrated approach to the stimulation of entrepreneurship education.

Current activities promoting entrepreneurship in Italy only reach a small percentage of the student population. Most activities initiated remain largely extracurricular for university students. More importantly the effects of these activities are not measured, making it difficult to ascertain if these activities achieve their goals. In this sense, there is a need to develop an institutional line of action in order to establish a role for entrepreneurship education within university courses.

For a managerial point of view, the academic entrepreneurs lack managerial and administrative competencies. In this sense, it is important to organize courses on these issues in STEM courses. Another alternative is to include a manager or a surrogate entrepreneur (practitioners) in the foundation team. According to Ben-Hafaïedh, Micozzi, and Pattitoni (2018) the entrepreneurial configuration composed of academics and practitioners seems the most effective configuration in terms of commercial performance. This core entrepreneurial team configuration, together with a public research institution in the extended team, appears as the best fit if the objective is commercial performance. In another study I'm conducting, I have noticed that temporary/young academics act as "cognitive distance optimizers" with the non-academics in entrepreneurial teams and with managers and entrepreneurs outside the spin-off. From the point of view of practical implications, this could be interesting for managers of non-university firms that can build relationships and contracts with ASOs more easily due to the fact that the dialogue is facilitated by these intermediary figures. This is especially true if we consider the relationship with small and medium enterprises in lower tech sectors that have a lower absorptive capacity, that is the ability of a firm to recognize the value of new, external information, assimilate it and apply it to commercial ends. Absorptive capacity refers not only to the acquisition or assimilation of information by an organization, but also to the organization's ability to exploit it (Cohen & Levinthal, 1990).

Moreover, policymakers may take specific actions to highlight entrepreneurs and shape cultural perceptions.

The data on entrepreneurial attitudes and entrepreneurial perceptions presented in the last Gem report shows that fear of failure was lower among those who saw good opportunities to start a business compared with the population in general. This suggests that it could be possible to improve perceptions about opportunities and increase intentions to start businesses by reducing fear of failure. Policy changes may have a positive influence on risk propensity: for example, reducing the large firm employment advantage with respect to health care and pension benefits or reducing the welfare state arrangements. Strong measures to protect citizens, in fact, may reduce incentives for entrepreneurship, even when individuals have favourable perceptions of entrepreneurship. For this reason, although attitudes and perceptions about entrepreneurship are fairly high, this is not matched by high intentions for starting businesses.

Moreover, an entrepreneurial culture may be reinforced by status perceptions that society confers on entrepreneurs, leading people to think that being an entrepreneur is an attractive pursuit. Media can also reinforce notions about entrepreneurs: for example, magazines or television shows can highlight entrepreneurs, or newspaper stories can feature the achievements of such individuals. Entrepreneurs as heroes, and their stories of success, can shape a society's impressions significantly.

This book offers interesting indications to policymakers. Stimulating innovative entrepreneurship is one of the highest priorities in the current economic debate, and is particularly important in countries like Italy, where economic growth is slow and youth unemployment rates are very high.

To foster entrepreneurship in Italy there is a lack of tax incentives and private investments, but first of all there is no adequate entrepreneurial culture. On the one hand, an intuition and a winning idea by themselves do not hold up unless accompanied along the corporate path by a strong business model. On the other hand, if there is a continuous shortage of resources and investments, this is revealed in a hidden lack of trust and orientation for innovation in the Italian market.

Empirical evidence shows that the industrial model based on small and medium-sized enterprises and concentrated in traditional sectors has experienced increasing difficulties in recent years in maintaining the competitiveness of the system and this requires an in-depth study of the causes that led to the decline in entrepreneurial activation rates in Italy in recent years.

The analysis of the characteristics and peculiarities of knowledge-based companies is therefore necessary to provide policymakers with useful data to undertake systematic actions aimed at increasing entrepreneurial activation rates, spreading the entrepreneurial culture in the territory. The main target to which efforts are directed is that of young people with high levels of education. This latter conclusion seems reasonably supported by several reasons: (a) for this segment of the population, the gap in entrepreneurial activation rates seems to be more marked than in other advanced countries; (b) these people are more likely to be able to activate initiatives with a high innovation content and in sectors other than those prevalent in the Italian industrial system.

In accordance with the results of Audretsch and Lehmann (2005), the new high-tech companies, in their location decisions, are not only influenced by traditional regional characteristics (level of development, presence of other companies, access to credit) but also by the possibility of accessing the knowledge generated by universities.

The impact of university production on new companies, however, depends on the spillover mechanism used to access that knowledge.

Entrepreneurship therefore thrives if policymakers support the transition between research conducted within universities and the entrepreneurial ecosystem and surrounding innovation.

An increase in the funds earmarked for the university would improve research activity and enhance the creation of knowledge spillovers. Regional policies can instead reduce the costs of locating close to universities through incentive mechanisms or by providing funding notices that promote collaboration between businesses and universities.

Bibliography

Audretsch, D. B., & Lehmann, E. E. (2005). Does the knowledge spillover theory of entrepreneurship hold for regions? *Research Policy, 34*(8), 1191–1202.

Ben-Hafaïedh, C., Micozzi, A., & Pattitoni, P. (2018). Academic spin-offs' entrepreneurial teams and performance: A subgroups approach. *Journal of Technology Transfer, 43*(3), 714–733.

Cohen, W. M., & Levinthal, D. A. (1990). Absorptive capacity: A new perspective on learning and innovation. *Administrative Science Quarterly, 35*(1), 128–152.

van der Zwan, P., Verheul, I., & Thurik, A. R. (2012). The entrepreneurial ladder, gender, and regional development. *Small Business Economics, 39*, 627–643.

Index

A. Micozzi, *The Entrepreneurial Dynamics in Italy*,
https://doi.org/10.1007/978-3-030-55183-4

The manufacturer's authorised representative in the EU is Springer Nature Customer Service Centre GmbH, Europaplatz 3, 69115 Heidelberg, Germany. If you have any concerns regarding our products, please contact ProductSafety@springernature.com

Printed and bound by CPI Group (UK) Ltd, Croydon, CR0 4YY
30/09/2026
02225475-0013